Get Ready for
Kindergarten

Jumbo Workbook

This workbook belongs to

Use pencils, crayons, and stickers to complete the activities in this book. Where there is a sticker missing, you will see this pattern:

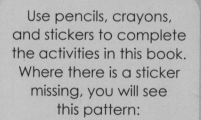

Dear Parents,

Welcome to the *Get Ready for Kindergarten Jumbo Workbook*!

Here are some tips to help ensure that your child gets the most from this book.

★ Look at the pages with your child, ensuring he or she knows what to do before starting.

★ Plan short, regular sessions, only doing one or two pages at a time.

★ Praise your child's efforts and improvements.

★ Encourage your child to assess his or her own efforts in a positive way. For example, say: "You've written some great C's there. Which one do you think you did best?"

★ Make the learning sessions positive experiences. Give prompts where they might help. If a section is too hard for your child, leave those pages until he or she is ready for them.

★ Relate the learning to things in your child's world. For example, if your child is working on a page about rectangular shapes, ask him or her to find some rectangular objects around your home.

★ There are stickers to use throughout the book. They help build your child's hand-eye coordination and observation skills. Encourage your child to place the stickers on each page before starting the other activities. There are also extra stickers, which can be used as rewards.

★ At the base of each page is a note for the parent. This note is intended to give you suggestions for building on the learning opportunities available.

Together, the activities in the workbook help build a solid understanding of core learning concepts to ensure your child is ready for kindergarten.

We wish your child hours of enjoyment with this fun workbook!

Scholastic Early Learning

Picture credits: All images courtesy of **Shutterstock**, unless noted as follows:
Tiew.Zog.Zag/Shutterstock.com: 68tr (kite); **Dziewul/Shutterstock.com:** 188tm (people in raft);
Daria Nipot/Shutterstock.com: 225rm (library).

With thanks to John Deere.
With thanks to Houghtonwood Labradors.

Contents

Package delivery

Trace the routes the delivery people take to deliver the packages. Start at the big red dot.

TOP TIP Tracing is a helpful prewriting activity for your child. While this page starts simply with horizontal lines, the complexity of the activities increases through the book.

Spider webs

Trace the lines from the webs to the spiders.

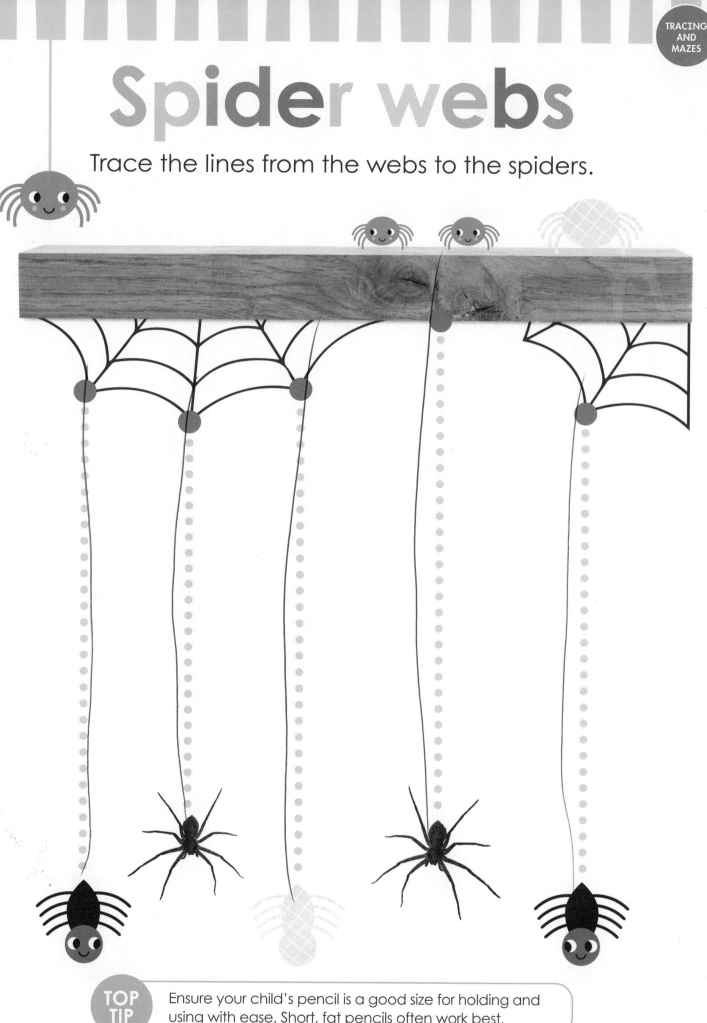

TOP TIP Ensure your child's pencil is a good size for holding and using with ease. Short, fat pencils often work best.

Cool ice cubes

Trace the ice cubes.

If your child finds holding the pencil difficult, ask him or her to hold a small object between the last two fingers when picking up the pencil. This frees up the pencil-holding fingers.

Sparkly gems

Trace the gems.

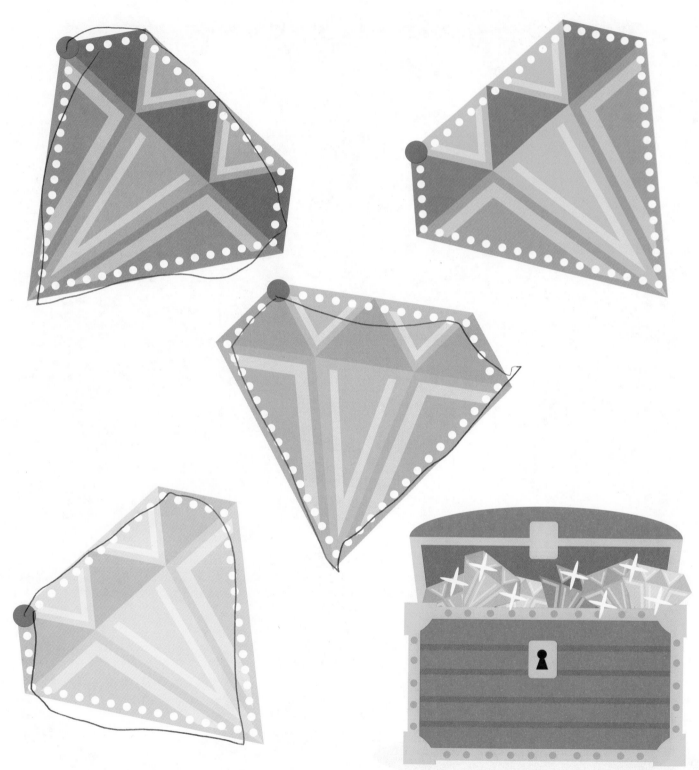

TOP TIP Starting on the big red dot prepares your child for writing. He or she learns to navigate the page from left to right, and from top to bottom.

Shooting stars

Trace the stars.

TOP TIP If your child finds this difficult, suggest that he or she does the first star in sections. Then suggest that your child keeps the pencil on the page for the second star.

Home, sweet home

Trace the lines on the house.

TOP TIP To improve your child's grip, try using triangular pencils, which help hold the fingers in the tripod position.

Sweet sunrise

Trace the lines to complete the sunrise.

TOP TIP Tracing boosts confidence. This sunset includes diagonal and curved lines. Praise your child on how far he or she has come.

Fluffy clouds

Trace the clouds.

TOP TIP Tracing develops hand-eye coordination and muscle memory. Once your child has completed this page, he or she could practice drawing curves on scrap paper.

Juicy oranges

Trace the oranges.

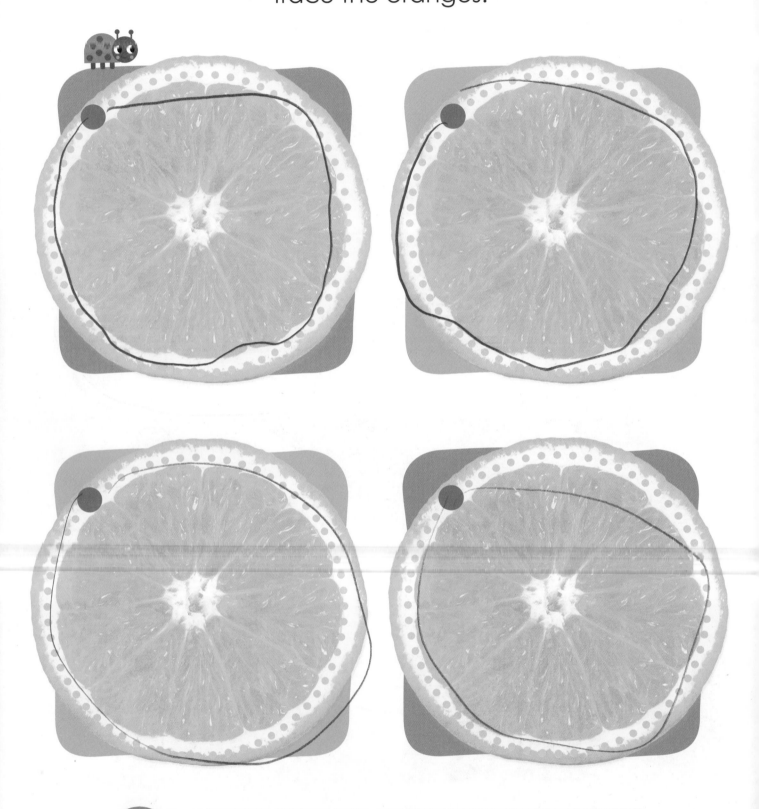

TOP TIP If your child finds tracing circles difficult, suggest he or she traces the outline with an index finger first to get a feel for the motion.

Cuddly kitten

Trace the spirals in the kitten and balls of yarn.

TOP TIP Starting in the center, trace the spirals outward, in a counterclockwise direction. This is good letter formation practice as most curved letters are formed this way.

Curly hair

Trace the loops inside the pigtails.

TOP TIP Tracing loops early in the prewriting journey familiarizes your child with creating the curves needed for neat handwriting.

Firework fun

Trace the zigzags around the firework.

TOP TIP Zigzags are important to practice as they prepare your child for writing w's, v's, and z's.

Hedgehog's home

Trace the trail to help the hedgehog get home.

Start →

Finish

TOP TIP
After completing the tracing section, your child is ready for guided trails. These help build fine motor skills. The goal is to keep the pencil on the page from start to finish.

Busy as a bee

Help the bee return to the hive.

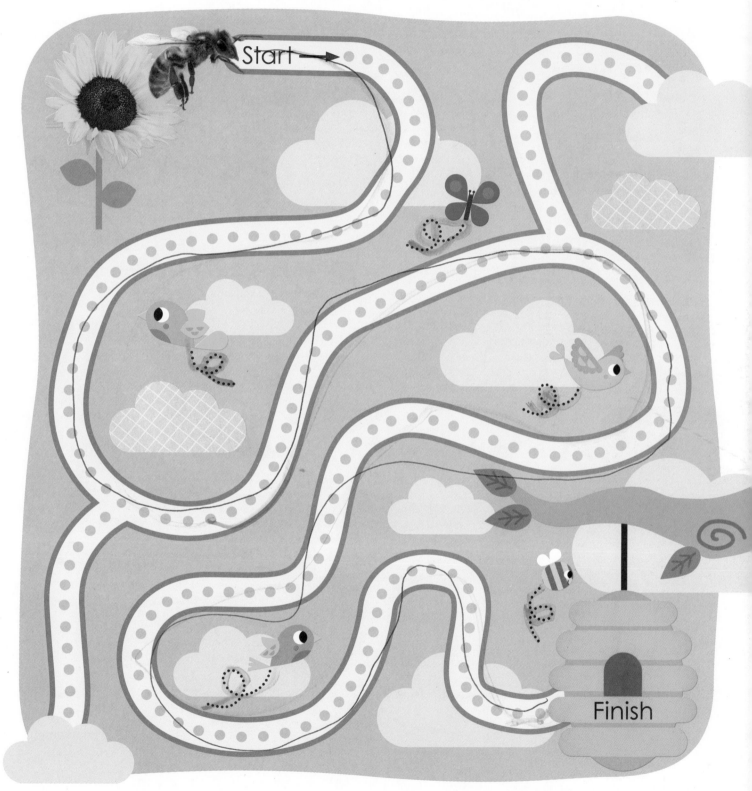

Start →

Finish

TOP TIP Guided trails prepare your child for completing mazes as he or she learns the concept of going from start to finish.

Roller coaster ride

Enjoy the ride from start to finish!

Start →

Finish

TOP TIP This guided trail is more complex. It incorporates loops, which help widen a child's sense of direction.

Bus stop

Help the bus reach the station.

Start →

BUS STATION

Finish

TOP TIP Before moving on to mazes, this gentle introduction to obstacles helps prepare your child for problem solving.

Anthill

Help the ants carry the leaves to the center of their nest.

Start

Finish

TOP TIP This page presents the first complete maze. Remind your child that going slowly will result in neater lines and fewer errors.

Butterfly flutter

Help the butterfly reach the flower.

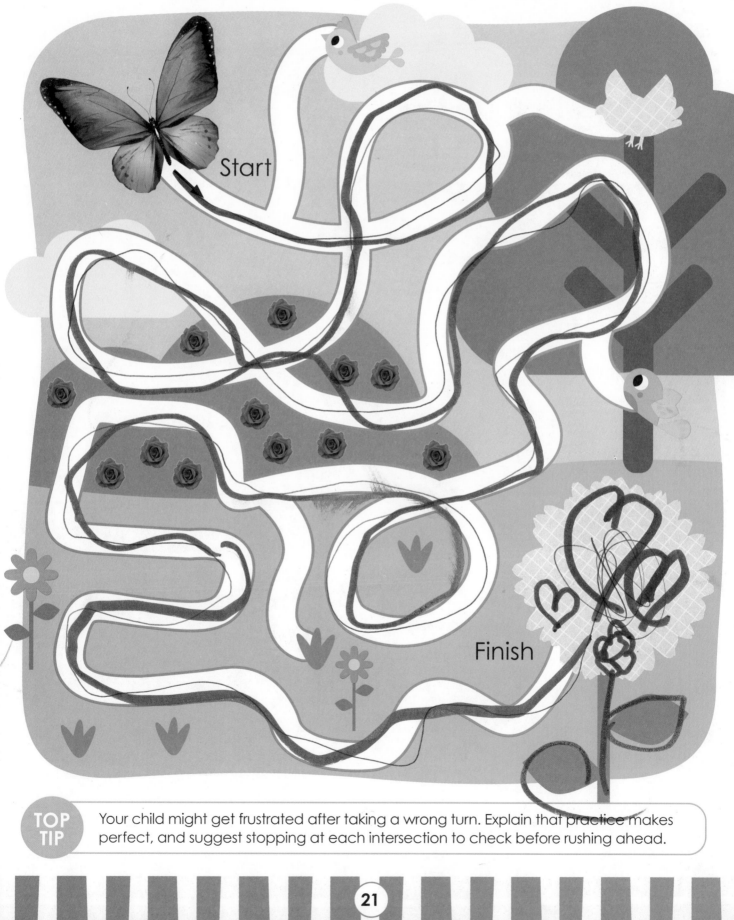

Start

Finish

TOP TIP Your child might get frustrated after taking a wrong turn. Explain that practice makes perfect, and suggest stopping at each intersection to check before rushing ahead.

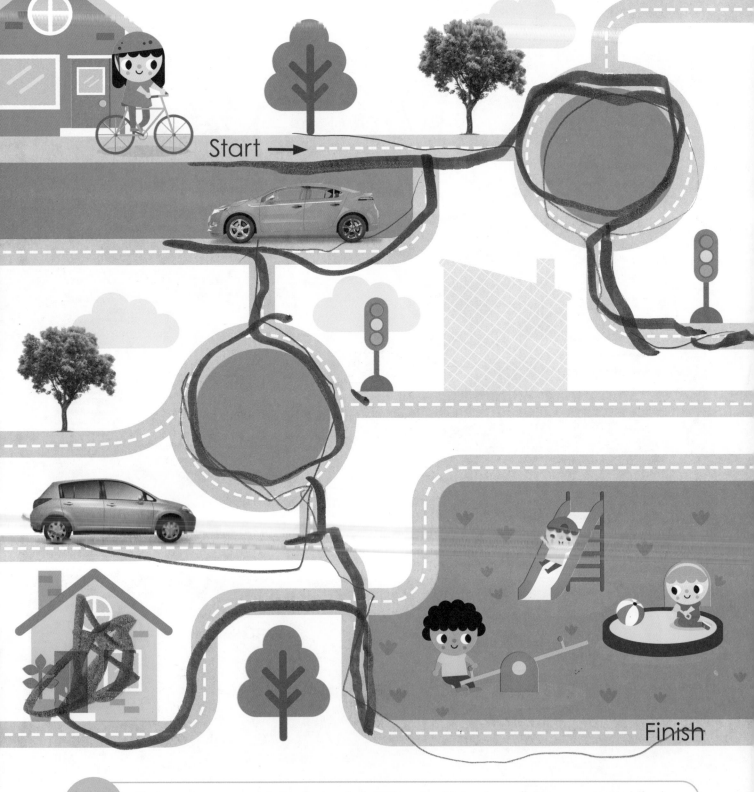

Bike ride

Help Charlie cycle from her home to the park.

Start →

Finish

TOP TIP To improve your child's sense of direction and boost confidence, suggest that he or she uses finger tracing to complete the maze before using the pencil.

Tidy up time

Help the trash collectors return to the recycling center.

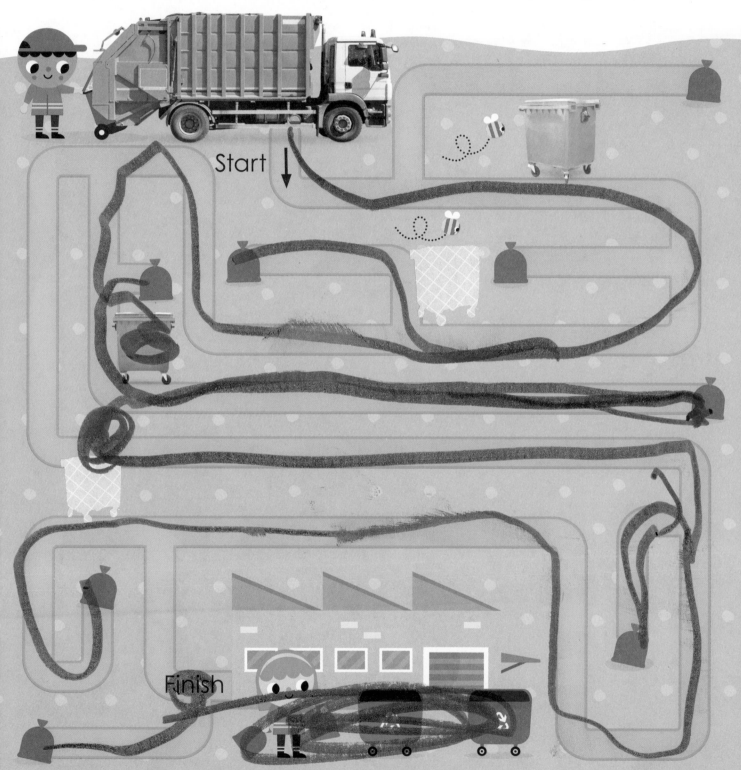

Start ↓

Finish

TOP TIP Completing mazes helps boost your child's persistence and patience as he or she works toward the end goal. Congratulate effort and perseverance.

Swim fast!

Help the turtle swim to the shore to lay her eggs.

Start

Finish

TOP TIP Suggest that your child scan the page before starting. This will help him or her form a mental overview of the task and end goal.

Leaping lily pads

Help the frog leap to his lily pad.

Start

Finish

TOP TIP Repeating similar activities, such as mazes, strengthens the neural pathways in your child's brain that are essential for learning.

Understand signs

Color the **stop** sign **red** and the **go** sign **green**.

Trace the signs on the store door.

TOP TIP Build your child's awareness that signs have meanings that help us navigate our environment more easily and safely.

Understand signs

Trace the exit and enter signs.

Color the restroom sign **blue** and the slippery surface sign **yellow**.

RESTROOM

 TOP TIP For your child's safety, help him or her learn the meanings of important signs and symbols in your local environment.

Be polite

Put a check by the child in each pair who is being polite.

Sticker the speech bubble into the classroom picture.

 TOP TIP Knowing how to behave appropriately will build your child's confidence and help him or her form positive relationships at school.

Be polite

Put a check by the child in each pair who is being polite.

Sticker the speech bubble into the picture.

TOP TIP Praise your child when he or she remembers to use polite language. This will help reinforce the behavior in a positive way.

Know emotions

Draw lines to match the children who feel the same way.

happy

sad

sad

surprised

happy

angry

surprised

scared

scared

angry

Children can communicate more effectively with others when they understand their own emotions and are able to read facial expressions.

Morning routine

Finish coloring the pictures to show Mia getting ready for kindergarten.

Mia gets out of bed.

She gets dressed.

She eats breakfast.

She packs her bag.

 TOP TIP Help your child understand that most people have a morning routine that they follow to prepare for a day at school or work.

31

Evening routine

Finish coloring the pictures to show Max's afternoon and evening.

Max reads his schoolbook.

He rides his bike.

He eats his dinner.

He takes a bath.

TOP TIP Let your child know that he or she might bring home a book to read from kindergarten. Encourage your child to look forward to this.

Movement words

Draw lines to match the children moving in the same way.

hop

walk

run

sit

jump

hop

walk

run

sit

jump

Food words

Trace the dotted line from each object to find its partner.

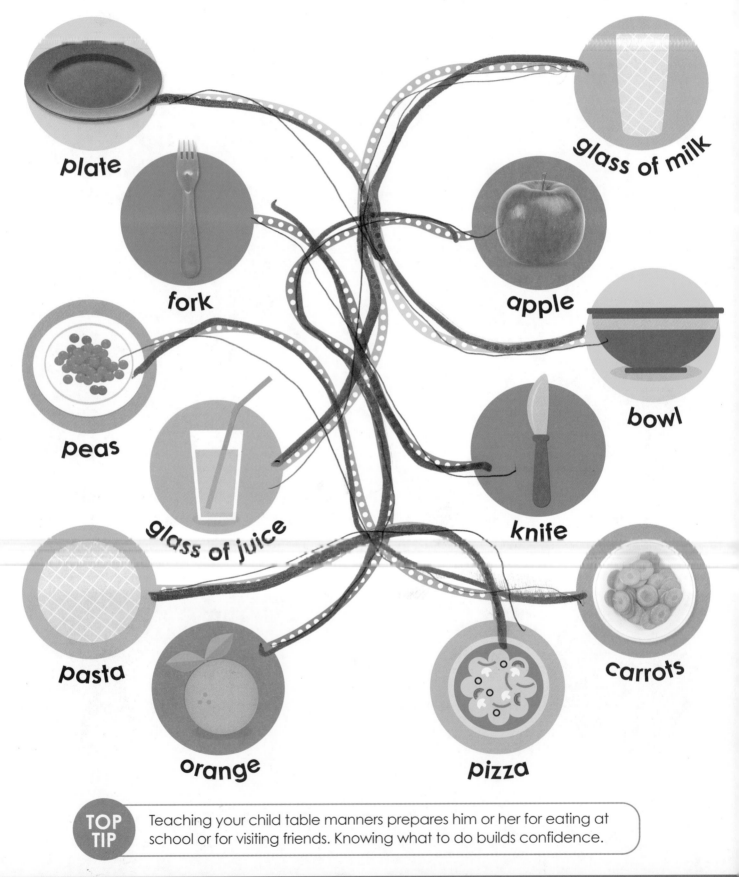

plate

glass of milk

fork

apple

peas

bowl

glass of juice

knife

pasta

carrots

orange

pizza

Teaching your child table manners prepares him or her for eating at school or for visiting friends. Knowing what to do builds confidence.

Time words

Yesterday Aria and Jack packed a suitcase.
Draw a picture of what you did yesterday.

yesterday

yesterday

Today Aria and Jack are going to Grandma's house.
Draw a picture of what you are doing today.

today

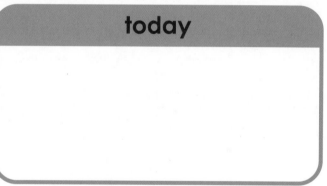

today

Tomorrow they will have a party for Grandma.
Draw a picture of what you will do tomorrow.

tomorrow

tomorrow

Brzaar
Hapeey

TOP TIP Use time words such as *yesterday*, *today*, and *tomorrow* in conversation so that your child becomes familiar with them and begins to use them.

Days of the week

Add the missing stickers to the days of the week.

Days of the Week

| |
| YOY |
| Tuesday |
| YOY |
| Thursday |
| YOY |
| Saturday |
| Sunday |

What day is it today? Circle the day with an **orange** pencil.

What day was it yesterday? Circle the day with a **yellow** pencil.

What day will it be tomorrow? Circle the day with a **red** pencil.

TOP TIP Discuss the days of the week with your child, talking about what your family does on the different days.

Months of the year

Add the missing stickers to the months of the year.

👓 Months of the Year ⭐

January	February	
April		June
	August	September
	November	December

What month is your birthday? Circle it with a **green** pencil.

What month are we in now? Circle it with a **blue** pencil.

What month will it be next? Circle it with a **purple** pencil.

TOP TIP To help build a sense of time, display a calendar where your child can see it, and allow him or her to turn over the months as they pass.

Weather words

Trace the weather words. Circle the word that matches today's weather.

sunny

snowy

rainy

windy

cloudy

TOP TIP Regularly discuss the weather with your child, encouraging him or her to tell you what the weather is like on different days.

Season words

Finish coloring the season pictures. Circle the season we are in now.

winter

spring

fall

summer

TOP TIP Throughout the year, talk about the current season and discuss what can be seen and felt in your neighborhood at this time.

Summer clothes

Cross out the clothes Emma won't need to pack for a hot summer vacation.

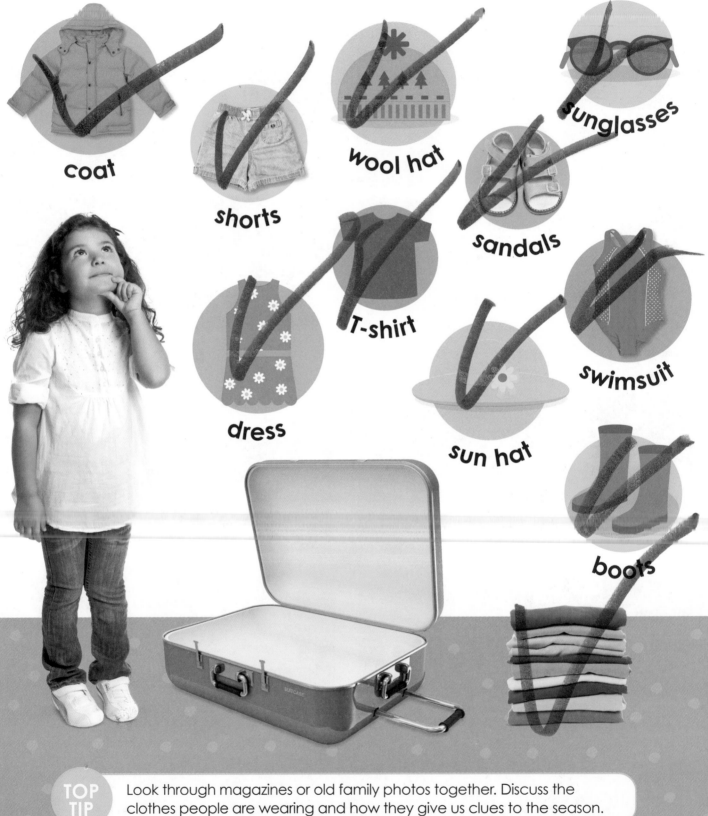

coat

shorts

wool hat

sunglasses

sandals

dress

T-shirt

sun hat

swimsuit

boots

Look through magazines or old family photos together. Discuss the clothes people are wearing and how they give us clues to the season.

Winter clothes

Cross out the clothes Dan won't need to pack for a cold winter vacation.

sweater

wool hat

sun hat

gloves

swim trunks

coat

scarf

sandals

When choosing clothes for the day, have fun by suggesting inappropriate clothes for the season. Then discuss why they might not be comfortable.

Size

The **pink** elephant is **big**. Shade the even **bigger** middle elephant **blue**. Shade the **biggest** elephant **green**.

The **orange** fish is **small**. Shade the even **smaller** middle fish **red**. Shade the **smallest** fish **brown**.

 TOP TIP Play games where you ask your child to choose the biggest ball or the longest pencil to build familiarity with these terms.

Volume

The first glass is full. Draw juice in the other glass so that it is full, too.

This first pitcher is half-full. Draw juice in the other pitcher so that it is half-full, too.

This first glass is nearly empty. Draw juice in the other glass so it is nearly empty, too.

TOP TIP Reinforce this learning by giving your child a drinking glass and asking him or her to half fill the glass with water or to empty it.

Length

Circle the shortest object in each pair.

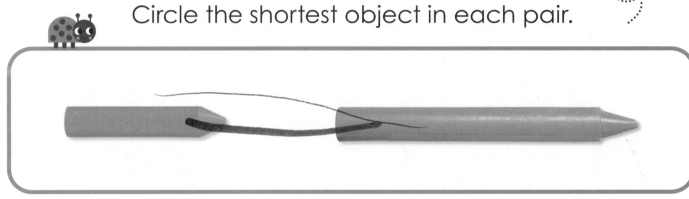

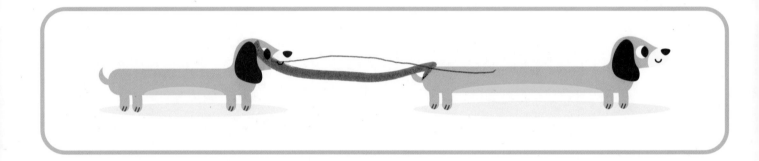

Color the last train car to make this train even longer.

TOP TIP Children learn by repetition, so once your child has been introduced to a new word or term, start using it in everyday conversation.

Height

Circle the shortest child in each group.

Tom grows a little taller every year. Sticker the correct age under each picture.

1   6   7   9

TOP TIP   Help your child observe the rate at which he or she is growing taller by creating a height chart and taking yearly measurements.

Lowercase letters

Lowercase letters are made of straight lines, curved lines, and dots. Circle the lowercase letters below.

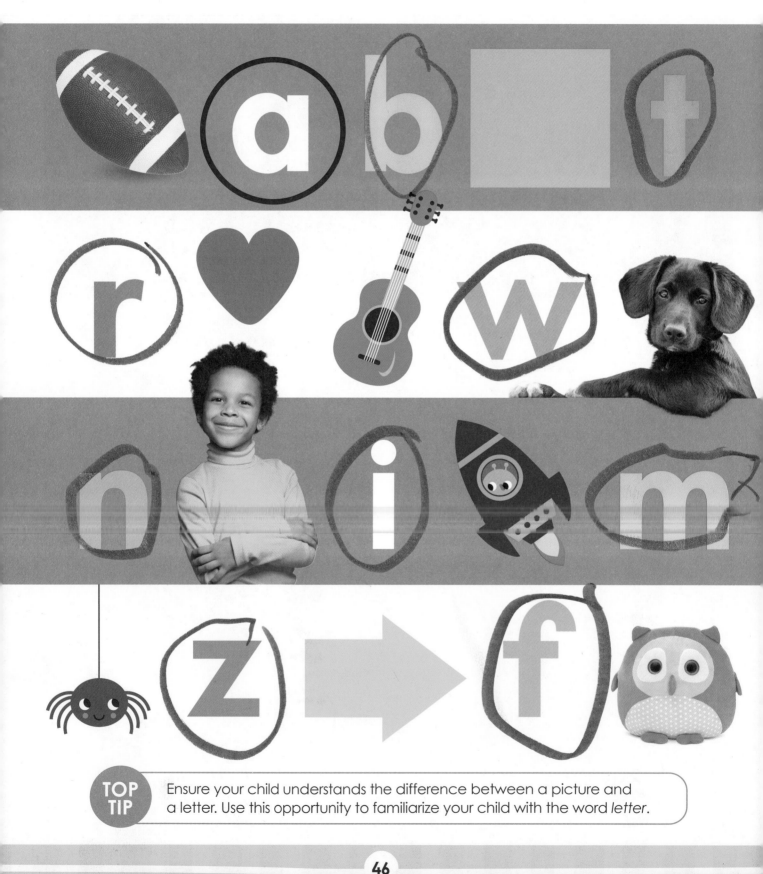

TOP TIP Ensure your child understands the difference between a picture and a letter. Use this opportunity to familiarize your child with the word *letter*.

Uppercase letters

Uppercase letters are made of straight lines and curved lines. Circle the uppercase letters below.

A C E F I Q S U W Y Z

TOP TIP Point out the straight and curved lines of the letters on this page so that your child learns that each letter has a specific shape.

What are words?

A word is made of a row of letters sitting next to each other. Circle the words.

girl

cat

home

jump

hello

star

pen

boy

TOP TIP Help your child understand that a word is made up of a short row of letters. Talk about the words on the page so your child learns that words are individual units of meaning.

Find more words

Circle the words.

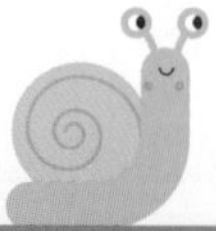

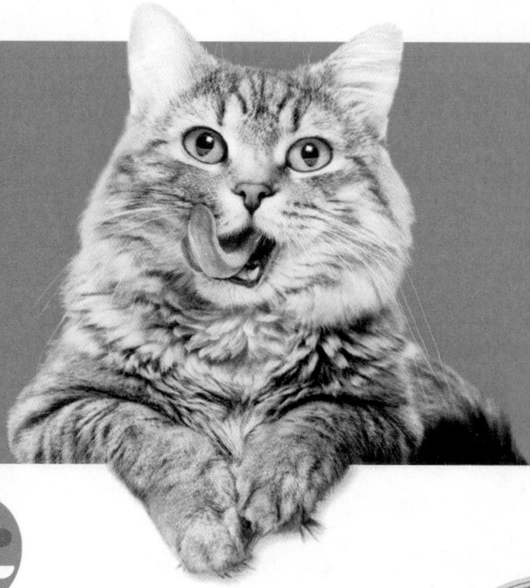

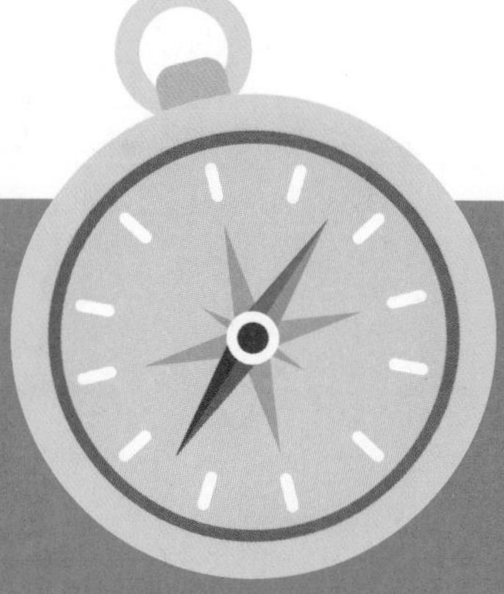

the

cow

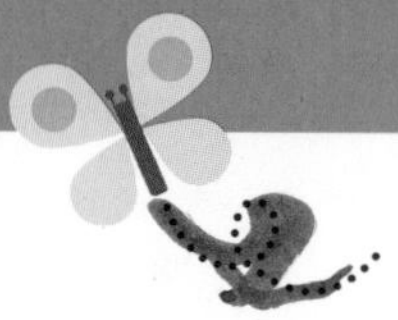

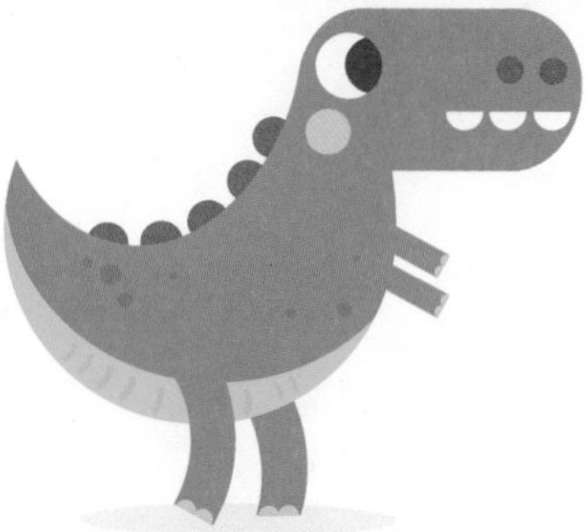

it

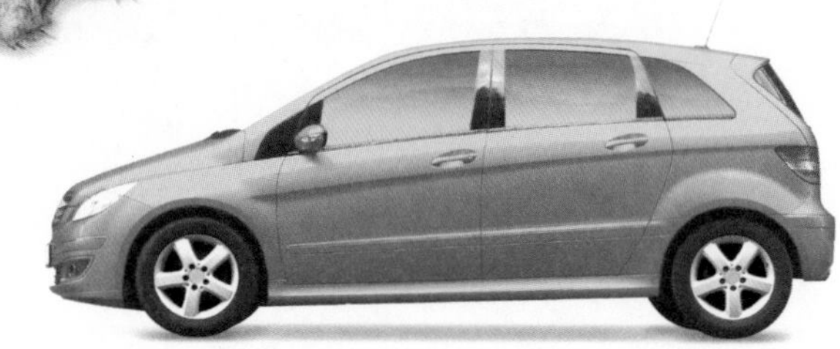

bed

stop

book

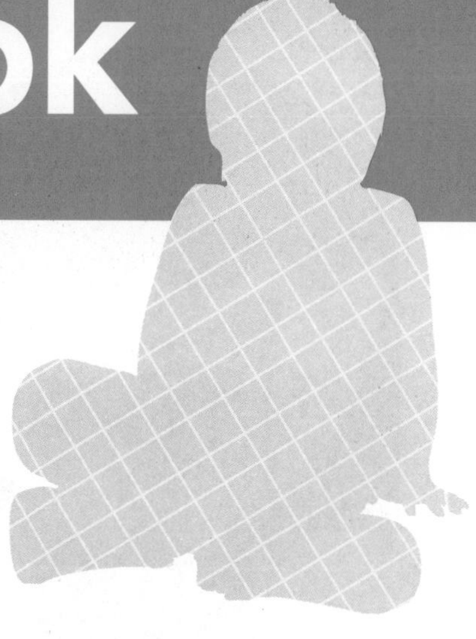

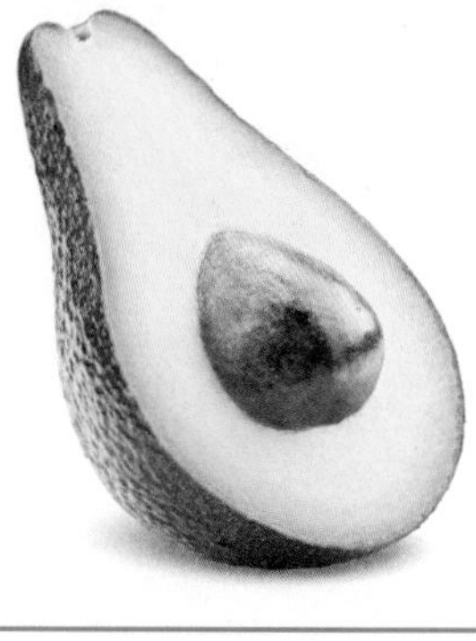

eat

pink

Letter or word?

Draw lines from the letters to the big L.
Draw lines from the words to the big word.

B

me

j

dog

L

Z

d

E

sun

fun

c

word

happy

H

g

sing

If necessary, look back at the previous activities to remind your child of the meanings of the words *letter* and *word* before explaining how to do this activity.

Match the pairs

Draw lines to match the lowercase letters.

Match the pairs

Draw lines to match the uppercase letters.

Match the letters

Find and circle the letter at the start of each word.

hat   o   w   ⓗ   t   n   q

van   l   t   u   b   v   w

boat   x   d   e   c   p   b

mug   r   m   w   n   z   o

egg   o   c   q   f   e   t

TOP TIP Use this exercise to help your child learn to focus on the first letter in a word and to practice matching letter shapes.

Match the letters

Find and circle the letter at the start of each word.

Kite   L M O K Z E

Ant   D A P V W M

Fox   H Q F X K I

Rug   T E B A P R

Gate   N G F Q O C

TOP TIP If your child is ready, point out that the initial letters on this page are uppercase, or capital, letters and that the letters on the previous page are lowercase letters.

Which way up?

Circle the letter that is the same way up as the first one.

A **Alice**   Ɐ   Ɐ   A   Ɐ

C **cat**   U   C   ∩   Ɔ

T **Tom**   T   ⊥   ⊢   ⊣

f **frog**   ɟ   ʄ   f   ⅎ

W **Will**   M   ⋎   Ɯ   W

TOP TIP   This activity builds awareness that each letter has a correct orientation. However, do not be overly concerned if at first your child writes some letters backward.

Cats and dogs

Draw lines from the words that say **cat** to the **cat**.
Draw lines from the words that say **dog** to the **dog**.

cat

cat

dog

dog

cat

cat

dog

dog

TOP TIP Help your child notice that the word *dog* has both an ascender (a line extending above the middle of the line) and a descender (a line extending below the baseline).

Socks and shoes

Draw lines from the words that say **socks** to the **socks**.
Draw lines from the words that say **shoes** to the **shoes**.

socks

shoes

socks

socks

shoes

shoes

shoes

socks

TOP TIP Point out that both words start and end with the letter *s* but they have different letters in the middle.

Letter order

Circle the word with the letters in the same order as the first one.

cup — puc   pcu   **cup**

web — web   bew   wbe

box — xbo   obx   box

bag — gab   bag   bga

sip — hip   ips   sip

Letter order

Circle the word with the letters in the same order as the first one.

crab — carb   crab   brac

ship — hips   pihs   ship

frog — frog   grof   forg

brush — shubr   brush   bushr

shell — shlel   lselh   shell

TOP TIP If your child finds this difficult, ask him or her to start by looking at the first letter and crossing out the options that don't begin with the correct first letter.

Write the words

Use the pictures to help you read the words.
Then the trace the words.

fan   jet   log

dig   pup   hen

TOP TIP At this stage, do not expect your child to be able to sound out the words. Instead, ensure he or she understands that each tracing word names the picture above it.

Write the words

Use the pictures to help you read the words.
Then the trace the words.

slug   bell   swim

chick clock flag

When children first learn to read, they use the pictures as clues to the words' meanings. Over time, they come to rely more heavily on sounding out the letters.

What is a sentence?

We join words in rows to make sentences.
Trace the sentences.

I see a ball.

I see a wall.

I see a bee.

I see a tree.

TOP TIP Help your child notice that the words, or parts of words, that sound the same are spelled with the same letters.

Write sentences

Trace the sentences.

Here is a cap.

Here is a map.

Here is a boat.

Here is a goat.

TOP TIP If your child is ready, point out that a sentence starts with an uppercase, or capital, letter and ends with a period.

Trace the **a**'s, and say the words.

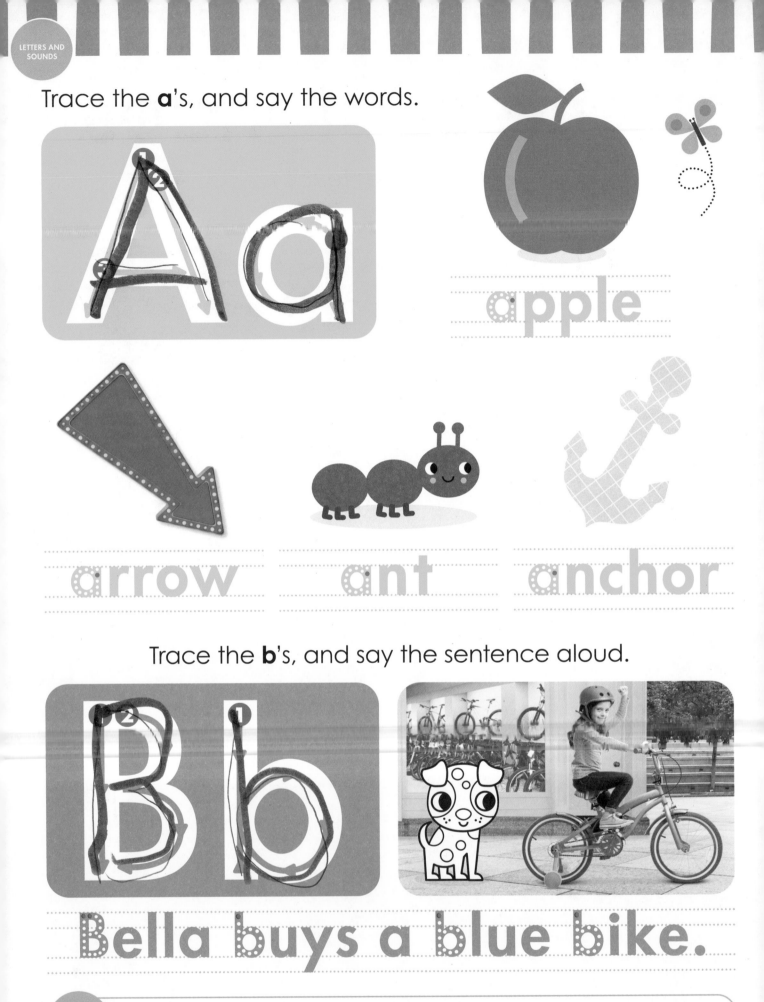

apple

arrow ant anchor

Trace the **b**'s, and say the sentence aloud.

Bella buys a blue bike.

Trace the **c**'s, and say the words.

cow

car   coat   cup

Trace the **d**'s, and say the sentence aloud.

Dave digs deep ditches.

TOP TIP Play I Spy with letter sounds to reinforce the learning. For example, say: "I spy with my little eye something beginning with *dih*," (*dog, desk, duck,* etc.).

Trace the **e**'s, and say the words.

egg

elf

elk

engine

Trace the **f**'s, and say the sentence aloud.

Flora feeds four fish.

TOP TIP The vowels (*a, e, i, o, u*) each have a short and a long sound. These pages focus on the short vowel sounds. (Long vowel sounds say the letter name. For example: *eagle, eat, eel.*)

Trace the **g**'s, and say the words.

goat

girl

ghost

gate

Trace the **h**'s, and say the sentence aloud.

Harry's hare hops home.

TOP TIP Build your child's awareness of sounds by drawing his or her attention to the different sounds around you. Ask what sounds can be heard and have fun imitating them.

Trace the **i**'s, and say the words.

insect

itch iguana igloo

Trace the **j**'s, and say the sentence aloud.

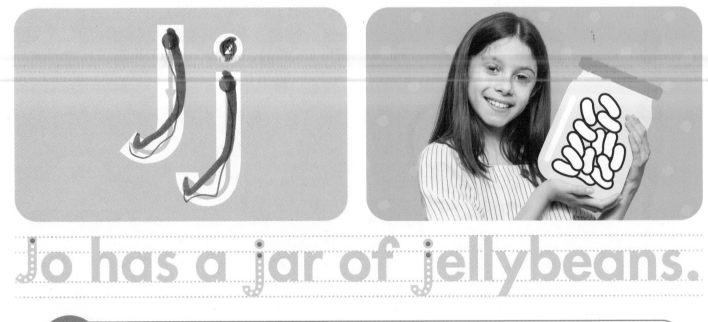

Jo has a jar of jellybeans.

TOP TIP Play games with letter sounds. For example, ask your child which word does not start with the same sound as others in a set such as *juice, jump, corn, jeans*.

Trace the **k**'s, and say the words.

kite

key koala kitten

Trace the **l**'s, and say the sentence aloud.

Liam likes lime lollipops.

TOP TIP Occasionally, stutter letter sounds to draw your child's attention to them. For example, say: Would you like a l-l-lemon or a l-l-lime Popsicle?

Trace the **m**'s, and say the words.

Mm

monkey

moon   mittens   mouse

Trace the **n**'s, and say the sentence aloud.

Nn

Noah notices nine nests.

TOP TIP Drawing out letter sounds such as *m* and *n* helps build awareness of them. You could ask your child to supply m words to finish this sentence: On my walk, I saw a mmmmm... .

Trace the **o**'s, and say the words.

octopus

ox   otter   orange

Trace the **p**'s, and say the sentence aloud.

Piper picks a purple pen.

TOP TIP   Have fun with alliterative rhymes, such as *Peter Piper picked a peck of pickled peppers*. You could also make up your own with the names of family and friends.

Trace the **q**'s, and say the words.

queen

quilt   quail   quiet

Trace the **r**'s, and say the sentence aloud.

Rose's ruby ring is red.

TOP TIP When you are out and about, point out words on road signs and buildings. Ask your child what letter sound a particular word starts with.

Trace the **s**'s, and say the words.

S s

sandals

sun   saw   seal

Trace the **t**'s, and say the sentence aloud.

T t

Tom takes a tasty tomato.

TOP TIP On car rides, choose a letter of the day. Your child's challenge is to find as many examples of that letter as he or she can on road signs, store names, and billboards.

Trace the **u**'s, and say the words.

under

umbrella   up   umpire

Trace the **v**'s, and say the sentence aloud.

Vivian has a violet van.

TOP TIP Ask your child to find the letter they are learning that day in their own home, for example, on a candy wrapper, a cereal box, or in the title of their favorite storybook.

Trace the **w**'s, and say the words.

wolf

wheel watch wagon

Trace the **x**'s, and say the sentence aloud.

Max visits six foxes.

TOP TIP Repetition is key to learning. Occasionally, practice the letters learned on previous days. Praise perseverance, and help your child understand that it will take time to learn to read.

Trace the **y**'s, and say the words.

yogurt

yell yellow yawn

Trace the **z**'s, and say the sentence aloud.

Zita sees zebras at a zoo.

TOP TIP Help build an interest in words by playing with onomatopoeia (words that sound like their meaning). For z, you could discuss words such as *zip*, *zoom*, *zap*, and *zigzag*.

Short a

Trace the **a**'s, and say the words.

bag

map

hat

cat

Circle the correct word.

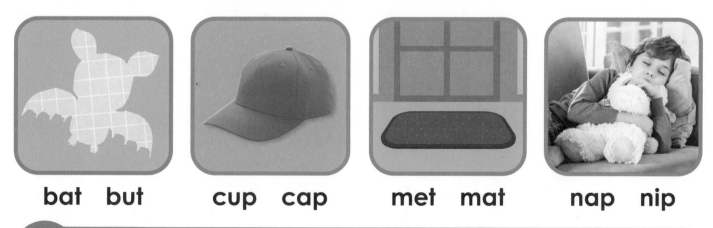

bat   but   **cup   cap**   **met   mat**   **nap   nip**

TOP TIP Blending beginning, middle, and end sounds is called decoding. Three-letter CVC (consonant, vowel, consonant) words are a good starting point for practicing blending.

Short e

Trace the **e**'s, and say the words.

bed

jet

hen

web

Circle the correct word.

net   not   **tan   ten**   **rid   red**   **gem   gum**

TOP TIP In the second activity, ask your child to decode both words. Help him or her notice that by changing the middle letter in each word, a different word is created.

Short i

Trace the **i**'s, and say the words.

rip

win

kid

bib

Circle the correct word.

sip   sap   **pug   pig**   **pin   pen**   **dig   dog**

TOP TIP Notice if your child ignores the middle or end sounds when decoding. Help your child learn to pay attention to the sounds at the beginning, middle, and end of a word.

Short o

Trace the o's, and say the words.

dog

box

pop

sob

Circle the correct word.

hot   hut   leg   log   pot   pat   hop   hip

TOP TIP If your child is unsure of a word, allow time for him or her to figure it out alone before providing a hint to help.

Short u

Trace the **u**'s, and say the words.

s u n

h u t

b u g

b u s

Circle the correct word.

cup   cap

hog   hug

bud   bed

pup   pip

TOP TIP You can make up quiz questions to build awareness of letter sounds. For example, ask your child what word we get if we leave off the *kih* sound in *cup*.

Lowercase alphabet

Trace the lowercase letters. Say their sounds as you go.

a b c d e

f g h i j k

l m n o p

q r s t u

v w x y z

TOP TIP Label objects around your home with lowercase signs, such as *bed*, *wall*, *table*, *door*, etc. Seeing the words regularly will reinforce the learning.

Uppercase alphabet

Trace the uppercase letters. Say their sounds as you go.

TOP TIP Using plastic letters or by writing letters on a page, create a game where your child matches upper- and lowercase letters.

What next?

Draw lines to show what happens next in each story.

1   2   3

1   2   3

1   2   3

TOP TIP Sequencing activities help teach the logical order of events. They help prepare children for creative writing, math, and science.

84

What next?

Draw lines to show what happens next in each story.

1

2

3

1

2

3

1

2

3

TOP TIP This activity encourages closer attention to detail than the previous one because all three stories involve baked goods.

What next?

Draw lines to show what happens next in each story.

TOP TIP Encourage your child to focus on details by discussing the differences in the three types of houses in this activity.

86

Sort and tell

Finish coloring the pictures. Then cut them out and put them in the right order. Tell someone the story of *The Three Little Pigs*.

TOP TIP Remind your child of the story of *The Three Little Pigs* before starting this activity. You can find text versions and videos online if you need them.

Sort and tell

Finish coloring the pictures. Then cut them out and put them in the right order. Tell someone the story of *Cinderella*.

TOP TIP This activity will be on the reverse of the previous activity. Ensure your child has the correct images upright before sorting.

Finish the story

Draw a picture to show what happens next.

 TOP TIP Discuss the details of each box, linking them with words such as *next* and *then*. Help your child come up with a logical ending.

Finish the story

Draw a picture to show what happens next.

TOP TIP — Discuss possible last images, such the dog shaking mud over the girl or the girl giving the dog a bath, but let your child choose what to draw.

Draw a story

Draw two pictures to show what happens in a story with these things in it:

a child   **a dinosaur**   **a spaceship**

What Happened First   ## What Happened Next

TOP TIP It may help to discuss ideas with your child before he or she starts. Ensure the second picture follows logically from the first.

Read and answer

Read or listen to the story. Then circle the answers and draw a picture.

My Ocean Dive

When I went diving,
I saw a cool animal.
It had a soft body
and eight legs.
It hunted fish.

1 Who is talking?

a boy   a girl   a fish

2 What animal is he talking about?

a shark   an octopus   a puppy

3 Where does the animal live?

in a tree   on a hill   in the ocean

4 Draw the animal in the box.

TOP TIP This activity introduces comprehension questions. At this stage, you will probably need to read the text to your child.

Hey, diddle, diddle

Say the rhyme. Then, draw lines to match the sentences with the pictures.

Hey, diddle, diddle, the cat and the fiddle.

The cow jumped over the moon.

The little dog laughed to see such fun.

And the dish ran away with the spoon.

 TOP TIP Nursery rhymes often tell short stories. Help your child to realize that each sentence in this rhyme describes a scene.

Buckle my shoe

Say the rhyme. Then trace the rhyming numbers and words.

1, 2, Buckle My Shoe

1, 2, buckle my shoe.

3, 4, knock on the door.

5, 6, pick up sticks.

7, 8, lay them straight.

9, 10, a big fat hen.

TOP TIP Rhyming texts help children learn to hear the syllables that make up words in preparation for reading and writing.

Good morning

Sing the song, and write in your name.

Good Morning

Good morning to you.
Good morning to you.
Good morning, dear ....
Good morning to you!

Good morning!

TOP TIP Let your child know that at preschool or kindergarten, the class may sing short rhymes together every day.

Wheels on the bus

Sing the song. Then trace the round wheels and the swishing wipers.

The Wheels on the Bus

The wheels on the bus go round and round, round and round, round and round.
The wheels on the bus go round and round, all day long!

The wipers on the bus go swish, swish, swish, swish, swish, swish, swish, swish, swish.
The wipers on the bus go swish, swish, swish, all day long!

TOP TIP You can add hand actions (circular motions for the wheels, and back-and-forth motions for the wipers) as you sing together.

A fish alive

Trace the numbers. Then sing the song and point to the numbers as you sing them.

1 2 3 4 5 6 7 8 9 10

One, Two, Three, Four, Five

One, two, three, four, five,
once I caught a fish alive.
Six, seven, eight, nine, ten,
then I let it go again.

TOP TIP Number rhymes provide a fun introduction to counting. Help your child learn to point to one digit for each number.

Teddy bear

Pretend you are a teddy bear and do the actions while you say the rhyme.

Teddy Bear, Teddy Bear

Teddy bear, teddy bear, turn around.
Teddy bear, teddy bear, touch the ground.

Teddy bear, teddy bear, reach up high.
Teddy bear, teddy bear, touch the sky.

Teddy bear, teddy bear, bend down low.
Teddy bear, teddy bear, touch your toes.

TOP TIP Action songs help develop children's coordination as well as encouraging them to listen carefully to the words.

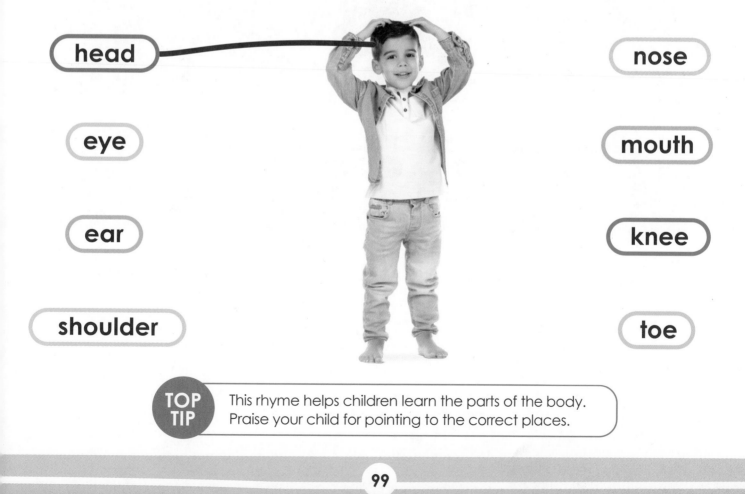

Knees and toes

Sing the song and use both hands to point to each part of your body as you go.

Head, Shoulders, Knees and Toes

Head, shoulders, knees and toes,
knees and toes.
Head, shoulders, knees and toes,
knees and toes,
and eyes and ears and mouth and nose.
Head, shoulders, knees and toes,
knees and toes.

Draw lines from the words to the parts of diagram.

head   nose

eye   mouth

ear   knee

shoulder   toe

TOP TIP This rhyme helps children learn the parts of the body. Praise your child for pointing to the correct places.

Row your boat

Sing the rhyme and trace the rhyming words.

Row Your Boat

Row, row, row your boat,

gently down the **stream**.

Merrily, merrily, merrily, merrily,

life is but a **dream**.

Circle the words below that rhyme with **stream**.

dream   cream   cat   team   beat   beam

TOP TIP   At this stage, you will probably need to read the words in the second activity to your child. Encourage him or her to listen for the rhymes.

Bingo

Trace the letters. Then sing the song and point to the letters as you sing them.

B I N G O

There was a farmer who had a dog, and Bingo was his name-oh.
B-I-N-G-O,
B-I-N-G-O,
B-I-N-G-O,
and Bingo was his name-oh.

TOP TIP This rhyme introduces the idea that words are made of letters. Ensure your child understands that the letters spell *Bingo*.

A

is for ant.

Color the **a**'s.

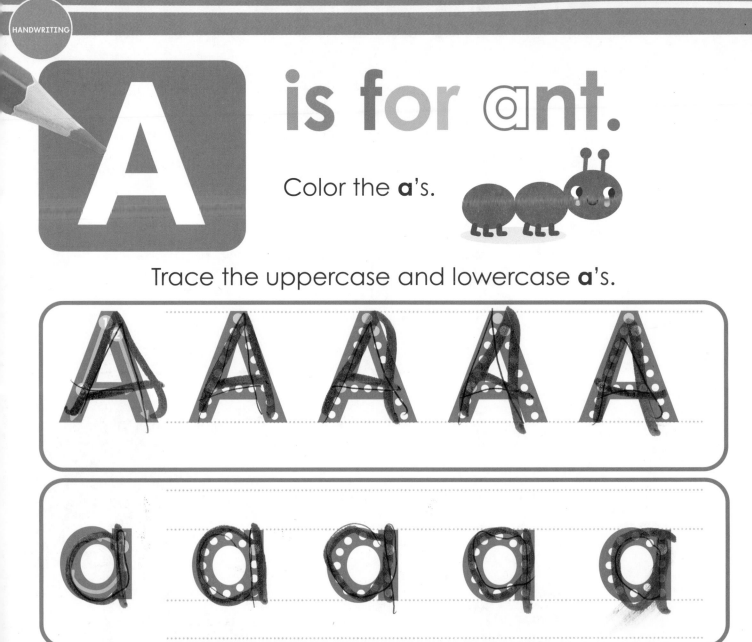

Trace the uppercase and lowercase **a**'s.

Find and circle the **a**'s in these words.

astronaut

alpaca

TOP TIP Make sure your child knows where to start each letter and in what order to write it. Forming good habits from the start will speed up his or her writing later on.

B is for boat.

Color the **b**'s.

Trace the uppercase and lowercase **b**'s.

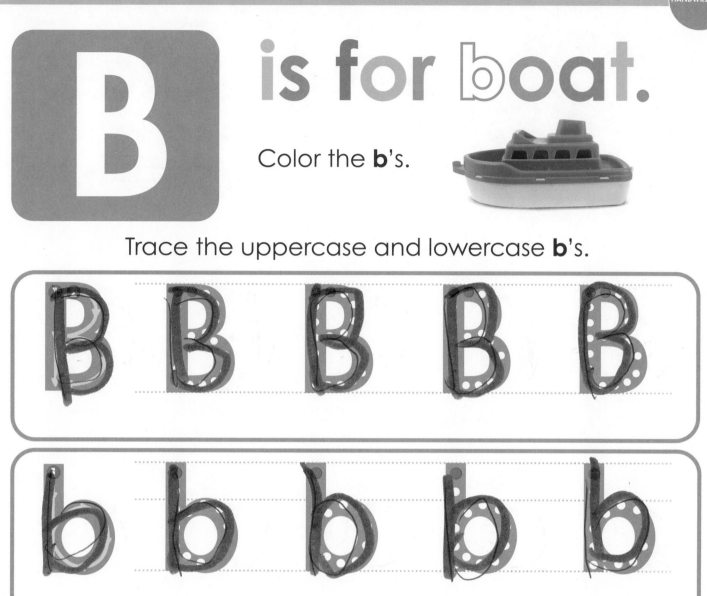

Find and circle the **b**'s in these words.

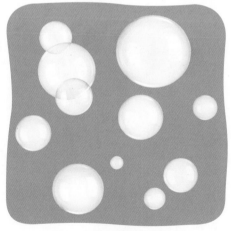

bubbles   **baby**

TOP TIP Activities that involve coloring between the lines help children build their eye-hand coordination and fine motor control, which both help with handwriting.

C is for cake.

Color the **c**'s.

Trace the uppercase and lowercase **c**'s.

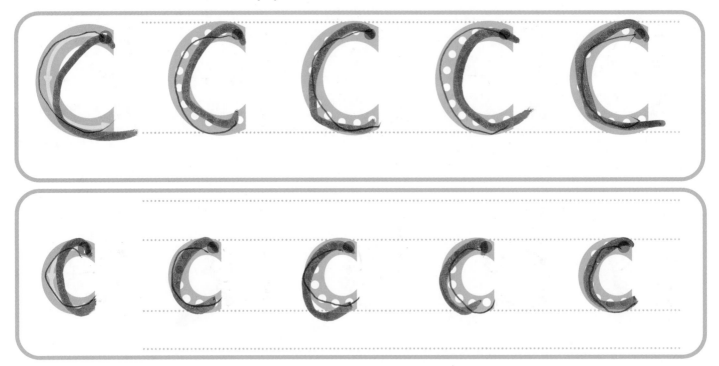

Find and circle the **c**'s in these words.

cactus

crocodile

TOP TIP Help your child hold the pencil between the thumb and index finger, resting it on the middle finger. (Very young children may have insufficient fine motor control to achieve this grasp.)

D is for dog.

Color the **d**'s.

Trace the uppercase and lowercase **d**'s.

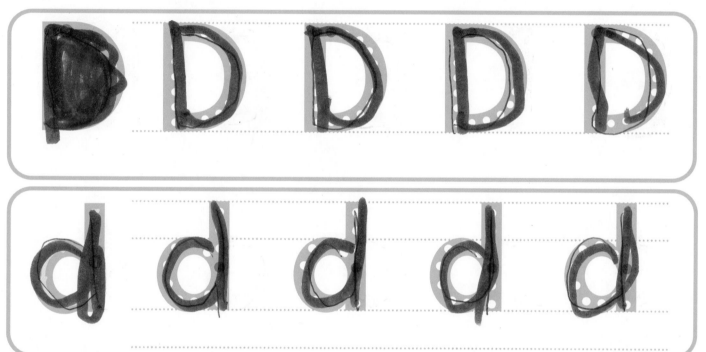

Find and circle the **d**'s in these words.

daddy

dodo

TOP TIP Point out that the letter d looks like a b with the stick on the other side. This helps build awareness that many letters have a correct and incorrect direction.

E is for egg.

Color the **e**'s.

Trace the uppercase and lowercase **e**'s.

Find and circle the **e**'s in these words.

elephant

envelope

TOP TIP Draw your child's attention to the shape of each letter. For example, say: e goes along in a straight line and then curls up and goes all the way around.

F

is for fox.

Color the **f**'s.

Trace the uppercase and lowercase **f**'s.

Find and circle the **f**'s in these words.

fifty-five

5+5=16
1+1=2
2+2=4
3+3=6

fluffy

G is for gift.

Color the **g**'s.

Trace the uppercase and lowercase **g**'s.

Find and circle the **g**'s in these words.

giggle

goggles

TOP TIP Make writing practice something to look forward to by allowing your child to choose a special pencil that is only used for writing.

H is for hat.

Color the **h**'s.

Hh i I

Trace the uppercase and lowercase **h**'s.

I is for insect.

Color the **i**'s.

Trace the uppercase and lowercase **i**'s.

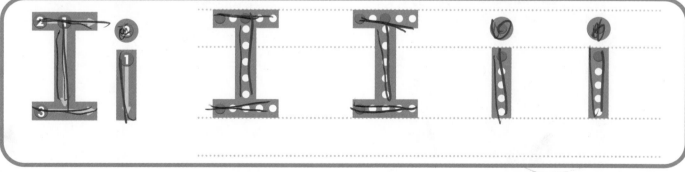

TOP TIP For i and j, make sure your child knows to draw the line first before lifting his or her pencil to make the dot. For speed, he or she should do a simple dot, not draw a small circle.

J is for jet.

Color the **j**'s.

Trace the uppercase and lowercase **j**'s.

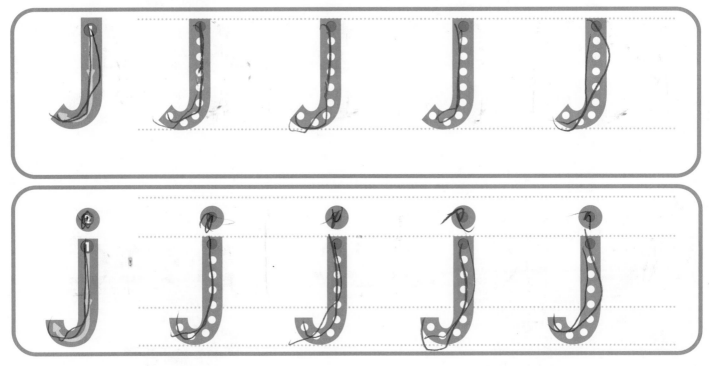

Find and circle the **j**'s in these words.

jumping jacks

jujitsu

TOP TIP Ensure that your child is holding the workbook or piece of paper with his or her non-writing hand to stop it from slipping.

K is for king.

Color the **k**'s.

Trace the uppercase and lowercase **k**'s.

Find and circle the **k**'s in these words.

kick

kayak

L is for lion.

Color the l's.

Trace the uppercase and lowercase l's.

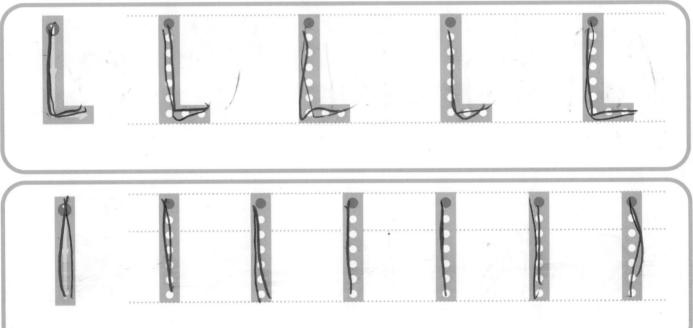

Find and circle the l's in these words.

lollipop

lily

M is for moth.

Color the **m**'s.

Trace the uppercase and lowercase **m**'s.

N is for nose.

Color the **n**'s.

Trace the uppercase and lowercase **n**'s.

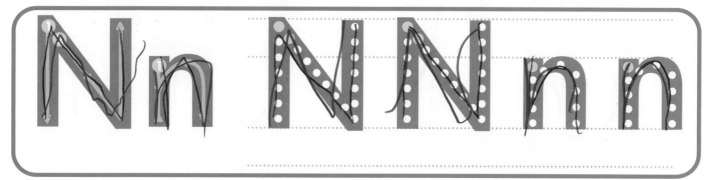

TOP TIP Ensure your child holds the pencil about 0.75 inch (2 cm) from the tip. Wrapping a rubber band around this part of the pencil can act as a reminder of where to hold.

O is for owl.

Color the o's.

Trace the uppercase and lowercase o's.

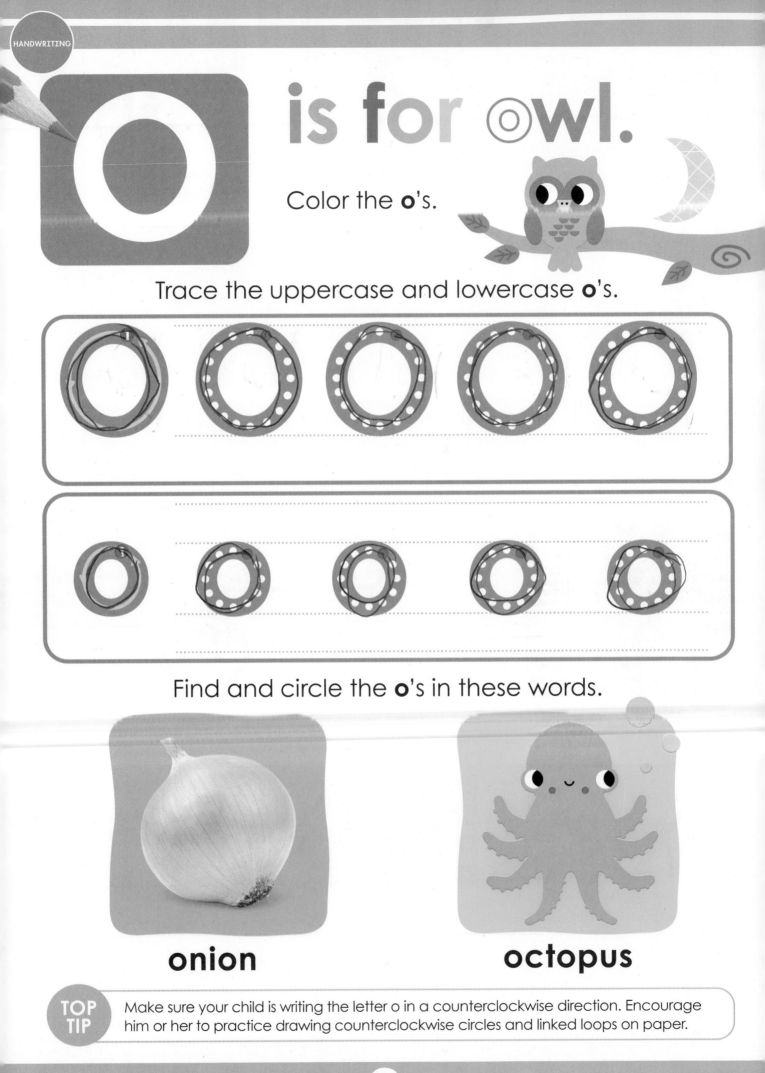

Find and circle the o's in these words.

onion

octopus

TOP TIP Make sure your child is writing the letter o in a counterclockwise direction. Encourage him or her to practice drawing counterclockwise circles and linked loops on paper.

P is for piano.

Color the **p**'s.

Trace the uppercase and lowercase **p**'s.

Find and circle the **p**'s in these words.

pumpkin

pineapple

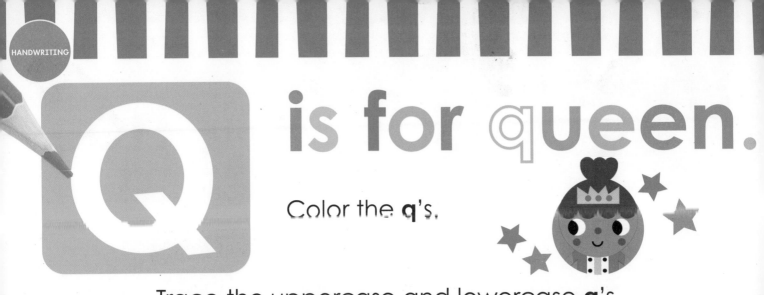

Q is for queen.

Color the **q**'s.

Trace the uppercase and lowercase **q**'s.

R is for robot.

Color the **r**'s.

Trace the uppercase and lowercase **r**'s.

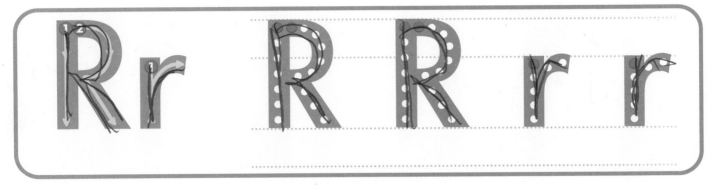

TOP TIP For right-handers, the page should be angled slightly to the left (counterclockwise), and for left-handers, it should angled slightly to the right (clockwise).

S is for socks.

Color the **s**'s.

Trace the uppercase and lowercase **s**'s.

Find and circle the **s**'s in these words.

scissors

seesaw

TOP TIP Provide your child with modeling clay to make letter shapes. You could write a large letter on a piece of paper for your child to use as a template.

T is for truck.

Color the **t**'s.

Trace the uppercase and lowercase **t**'s.

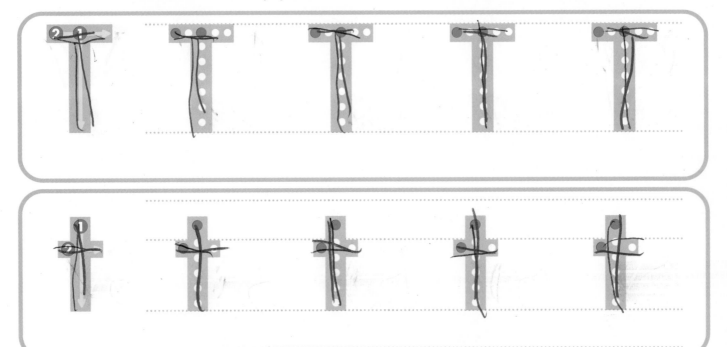

Find and circle the **t**'s in these words.

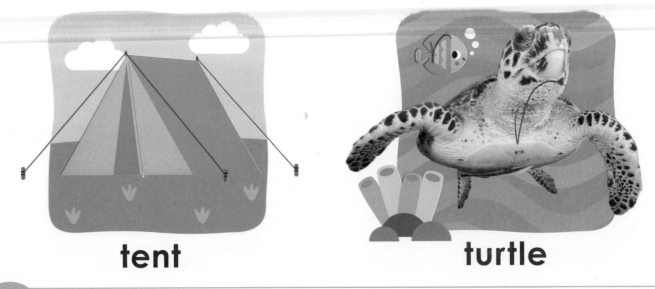

tent

turtle

TOP TIP Demonstrate how writing helps you. For example, let your child watch as you write a supermarket list. Allow him or her to cross off items as you put them in your shopping cart.

U is for unicorn.

Color the **u**'s.

Trace the uppercase and lowercase **u**'s.

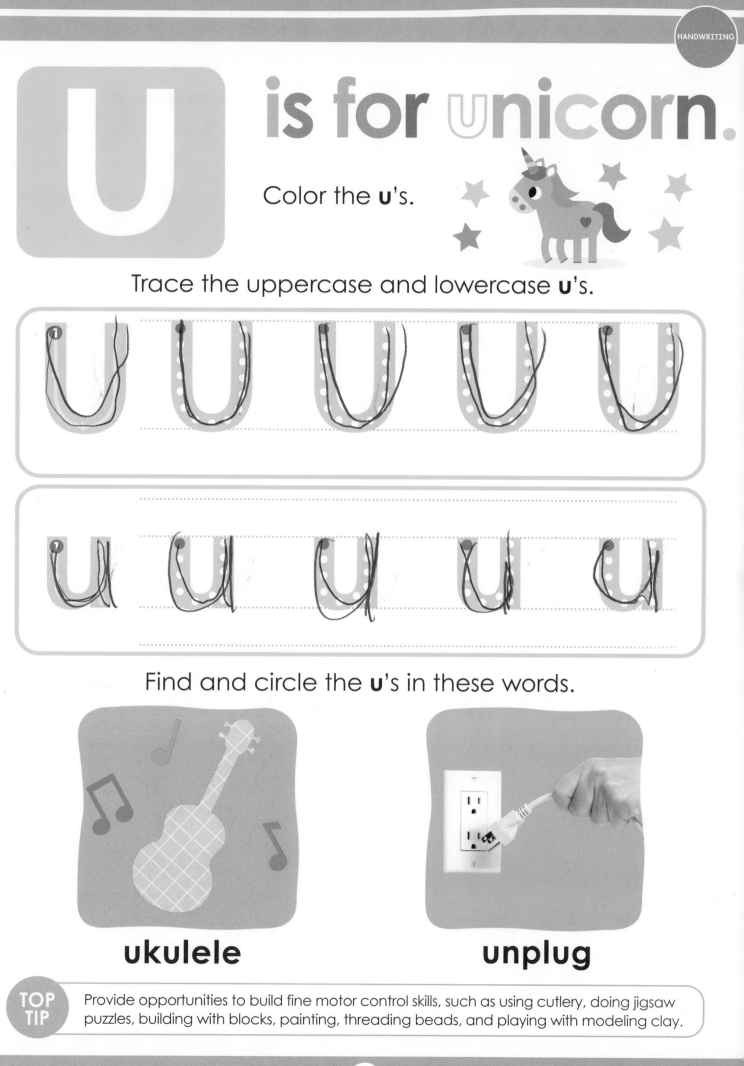

Find and circle the **u**'s in these words.

ukulele

unplug

Provide opportunities to build fine motor control skills, such as using cutlery, doing jigsaw puzzles, building with blocks, painting, threading beads, and playing with modeling clay.

V is for vase.

Color the **v**'s.

Trace the uppercase and lowercase **v**'s.

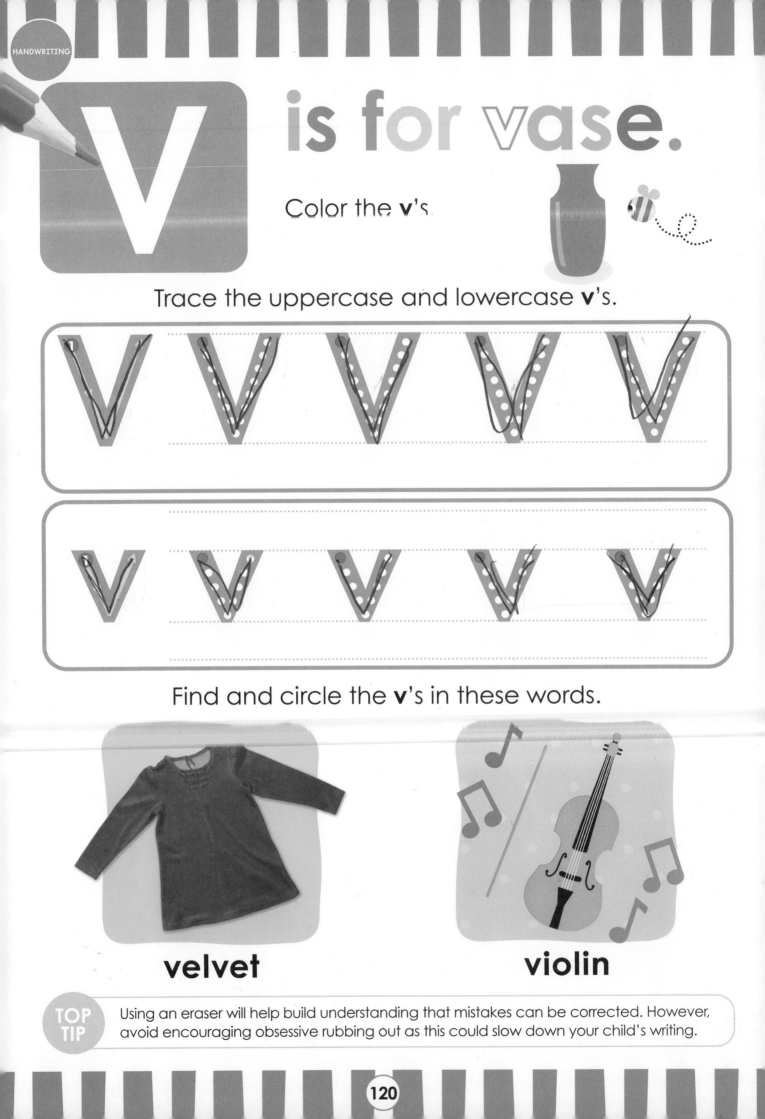

Find and circle the **v**'s in these words.

velvet

violin

TOP TIP Using an eraser will help build understanding that mistakes can be corrected. However, avoid encouraging obsessive rubbing out as this could slow down your child's writing.

W is for wand.

Color the **w**'s.

Trace the uppercase and lowercase **w**'s.

X is for X-ray.

Color the **x**'s.

Trace the uppercase and lowercase **x**'s.

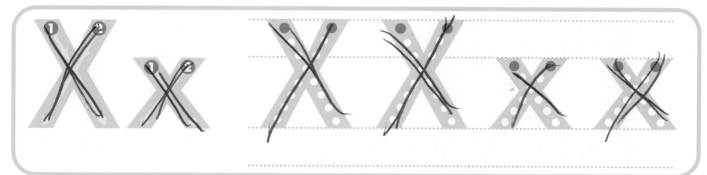

TOP TIP Provide opportunities for your child to practice writing letters in other places, such as in sand, mud, or on a misty window. Writing large letters in the air is also good practice.

Y is for yak.

Color the **y**'s.

Trace the uppercase and lowercase **y**'s.

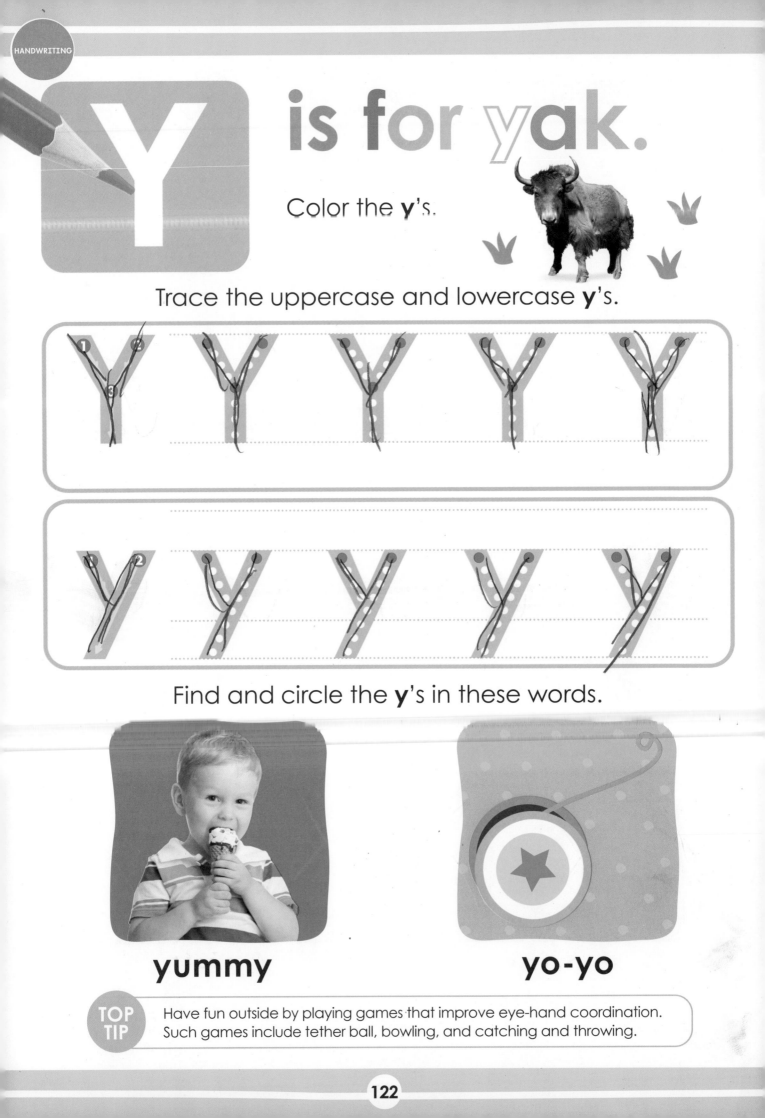

Find and circle the **y**'s in these words.

yummy

yo-yo

TOP TIP Have fun outside by playing games that improve eye-hand coordination. Such games include tether ball, bowling, and catching and throwing.

Z

Z is for zoo.

Color the **z**'s.

Trace the uppercase and lowercase **z**'s.

Find and circle the **z**'s in these words.

zigzags

puzzle

TOP TIP — Using large, light letters, write a short sentence about a topic of interest to your child. Allow your child to trace over it and then illustrate it with a picture. Display it on a wall.

Trace the **1** with your finger. Then trace **1** tractor.

one

Find and circle **1 blue** cupcake.

Trace the **1**'s with your pencil.

TOP TIP Help your child learn to trace the ones by starting at the top of the vertical line and moving the pencil downward.

Trace the **2** with your finger. Then trace **2** socks.

2

two

Color **2** birds.

Trace the **2**'s with your pencil.

2 2 2 2 2 2

TOP TIP Reinforce the meaning of two in everyday situations. For example, say: "Oh good, these two socks match. Can you find two more that match?"

Trace the **3** with your finger. Then trace **3** cats.

3
three

Circle the cone with **3** scoops of ice cream.

Trace the **3**'s with your pencil.

TOP TIP Count the scoops of ice cream together, pointing to the scoops and ensuring that your child says one number for each scoop.

Trace the **4** with your finger. Then trace **4** shells.

4
four

Find and circle **4** dinosaurs.

Mariah

Trace the **4**'s with your pencil.

4 4 4 4 4 4

TOP TIP Help your child understand that the written numeral four stands for the number of objects in each picture on this page.

Trace the **5** with your finger. Then trace **5** hearts.

5
five

Trace the numbers to count the starfish's **5** legs.

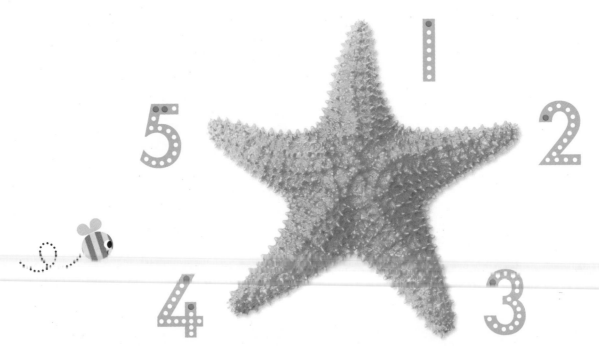

Trace the **5**'s with your pencil.

TOP TIP Build on the learning by counting how many fingers are on one hand or how many toes are on one foot. Count one finger or toe per number.

Count to 5

Trace the numbers. Then draw lines to match the numbers to the groups.

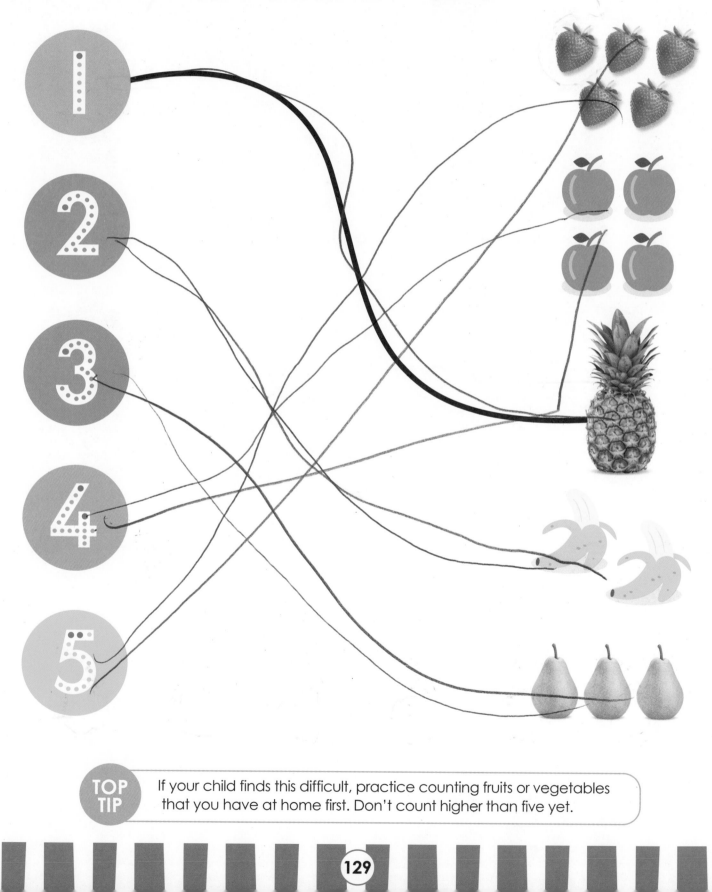

TOP TIP   If your child finds this difficult, practice counting fruits or vegetables that you have at home first. Don't count higher than five yet.

Trace the **6** with your finger. Then trace **6** jelly beans.

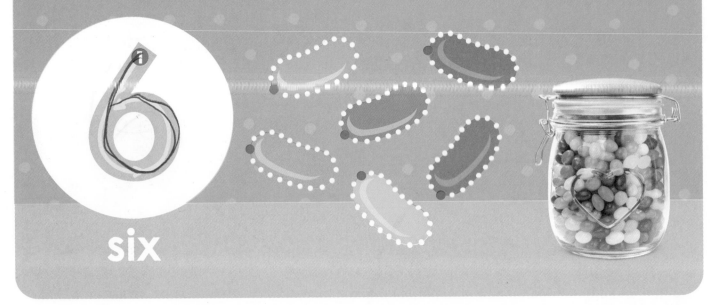

6

six

Color the balls **6** different colors.

Trace the **6**'s with your pencil.

TOP TIP Tell your child that insects have six legs. Look at pictures of insects (such as bees, beetles, and ants) on the Internet, and count their legs.

Trace the **7** with your finger. Then trace **7** hats.

seven

Sticker **7** butterflies into the scene.

Trace the **7**'s with your pencil.

TOP TIP When this page is finished, ask your child to count the butterfly stickers. Help him or her learn to point to each butterfly once and only once.

Trace the **8** with your finger. Then trace **8** apples.

eight

Trace the numbers to count the race cars.

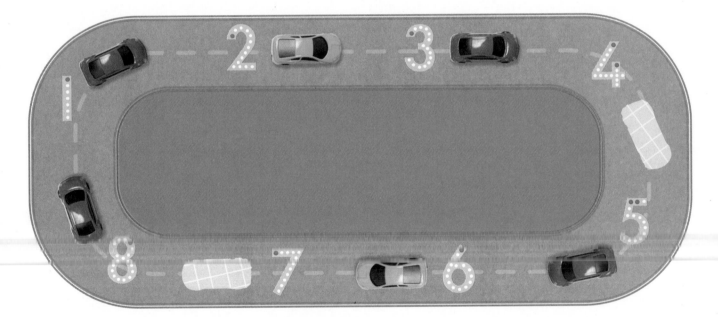

Trace the **8**'s with your pencil.

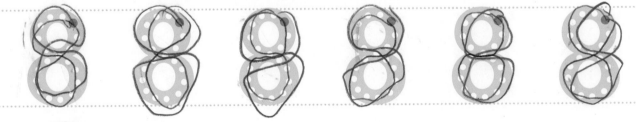

 TOP TIP After your child has traced the row of eights, ask which one he or she thought was the neatest. Discuss his or her reasons for this choice.

Trace the **9** with your finger. Then trace **9** smiley faces.

nine

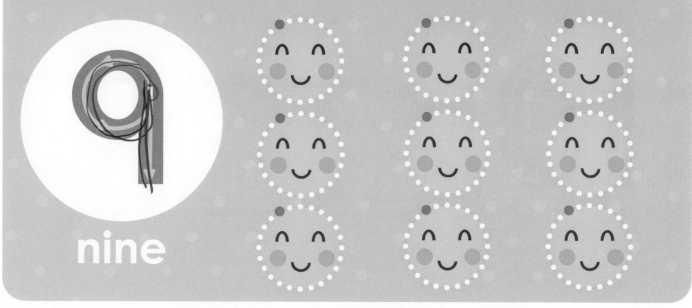

Circle the plant with **9** flowers.

Trace the **9**'s with your pencil.

TOP TIP Reinforce the learning by asking, "What number is this?" while pointing to single numerals on birthday cards, homes, and other places.

Trace the **10** with your finger. Then trace **10** stars.

ten

Sticker, color, and count **10** mugs.

Trace the **10**'s with your pencil.

10 10 10 10

Count to ten together using the fingers on both hands.
If your child is ready, try counting backward from ten to one.

Count to 10

Count the creatures in each row and write the number.

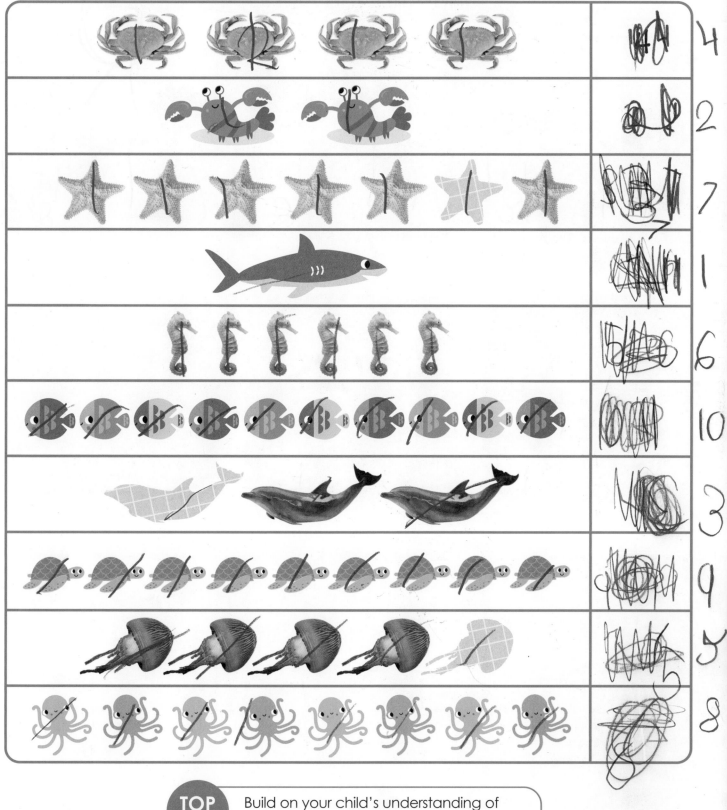

TOP TIP Build on your child's understanding of numbers by singing fun counting songs.

Change the order

Count the people or animals in each box
and write the number.

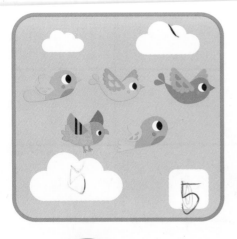  

Add one more

Count **2** trucks. Sticker **1** more to make **3**.

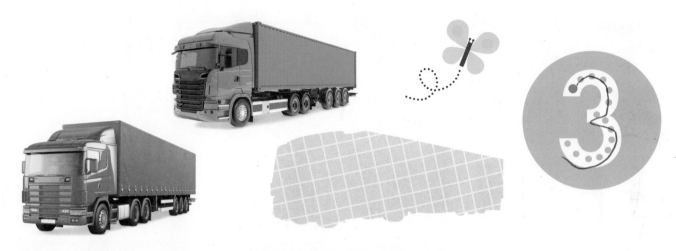

Count **5** sweaters. Sticker **1** more to make **6**.

Count **9** frogs. Sticker **1** more to make **10**.

Count from 11 to 15

Count **11** rockets. Color the last **1**.

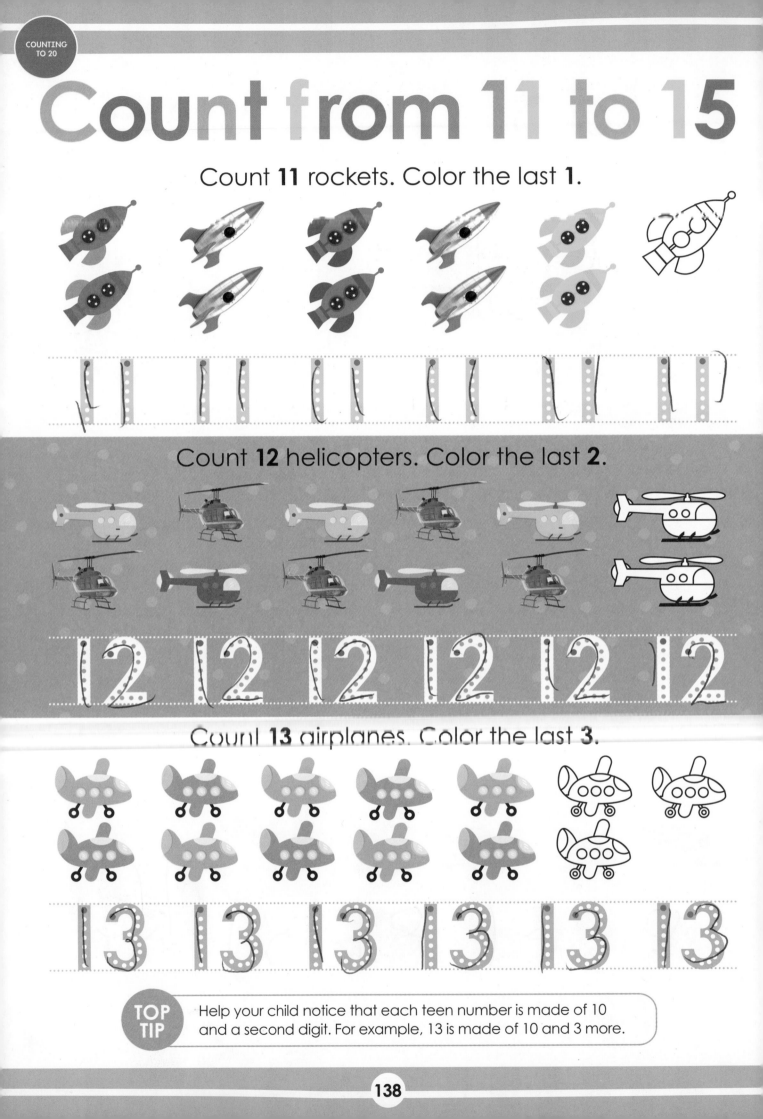

Count **12** helicopters. Color the last **2**.

Count **13** airplanes. Color the last **3**.

TOP TIP — Help your child notice that each teen number is made of 10 and a second digit. For example, 13 is made of 10 and 3 more.

Count **14** boats. Color the last **4**.

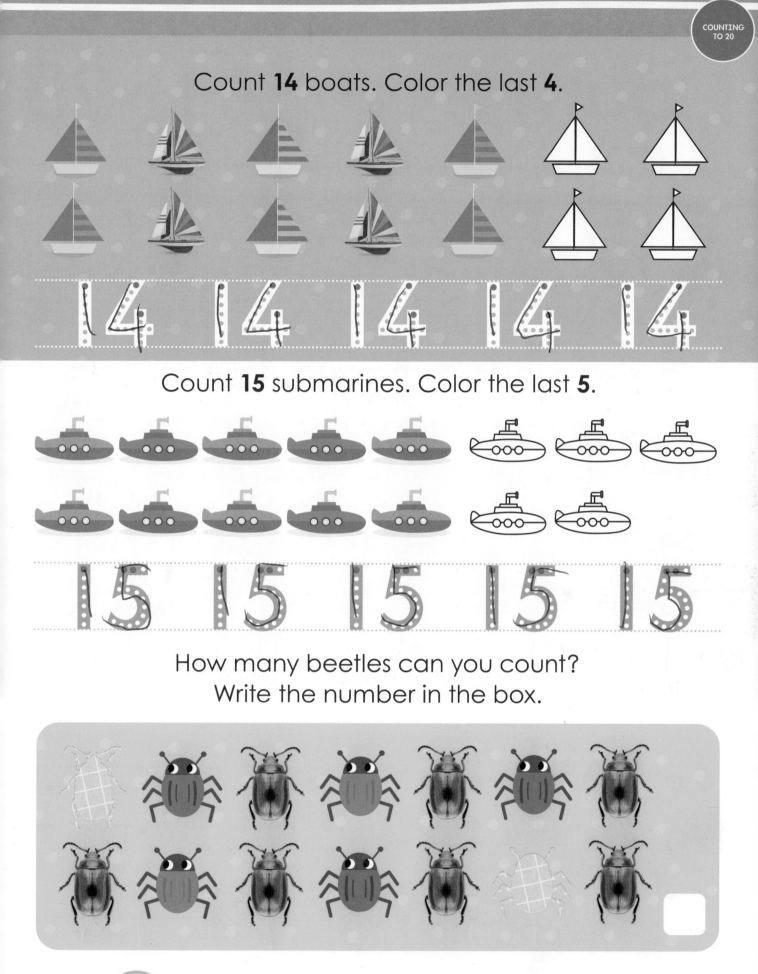

Count **15** submarines. Color the last **5**.

How many beetles can you count?
Write the number in the box.

TOP TIP If your child needs help writing numbers, refer back to the numbers traced earlier or write the number and let your child trace it.

Count from 16 to 20

Count **16** buses. Color the last **6**.

Count **17** vans. Color the last **7**.

Count **18** cars. Color the last **8**.

TOP TIP Tell your child that *teen* means *ten*, and then discuss how *sixteen* means *six* and *ten* and how *seventeen* means *seven* and *ten*.

Count **19** tractors. Color the last **9**.

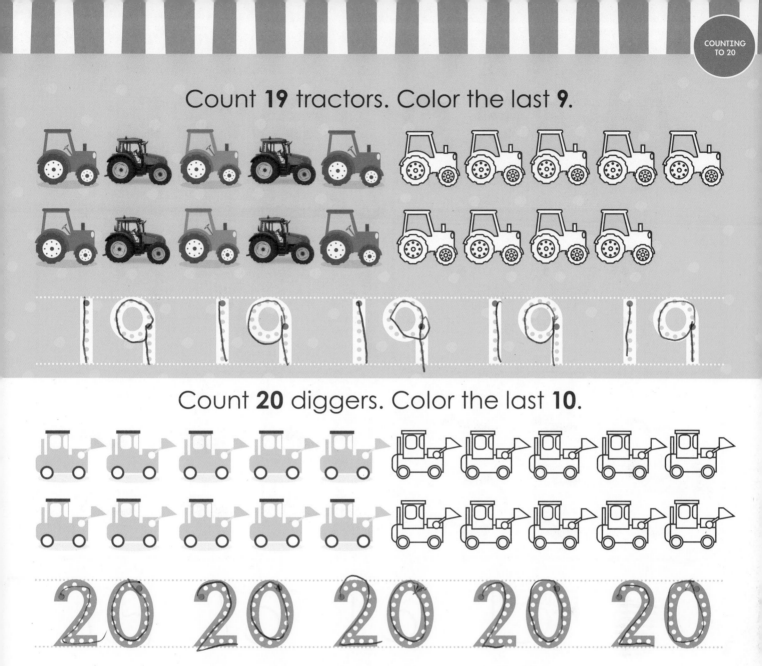

19 19 19 19 19

Count **20** diggers. Color the last **10**.

20 20 20 20 20

How many bees can you count?
Write the number in the box.

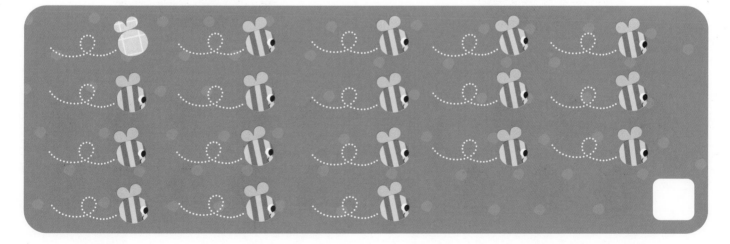

More or fewer?

Circle the biggest group in each pair.

Circle the smallest group in each pair.

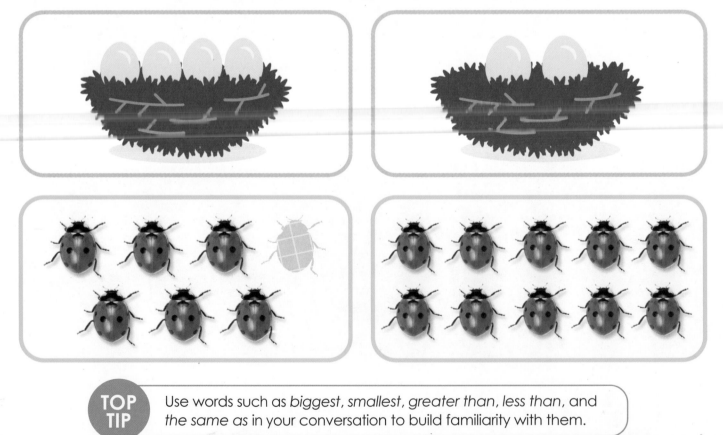

TOP TIP Use words such as *biggest, smallest, greater than, less than,* and *the same as* in your conversation to build familiarity with them.

Count to 20

Trace the numbers to count the lily pads.

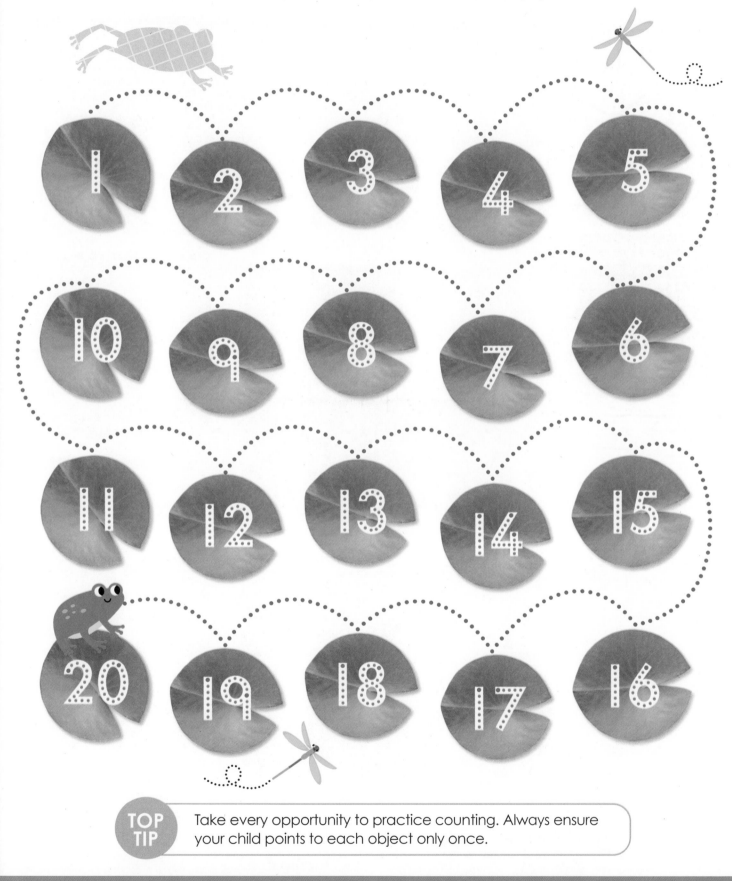

Take every opportunity to practice counting. Always ensure your child points to each object only once.

Squares

Find and cross out the object that is **not** a **square**.

TOP TIP To reinforce your child's understanding of shapes, ask him or her to search your home for other square objects.

Squares

Trace the **squares**.

Complete the **square** pattern.

TOP TIP Shape recognition will help your child form the building blocks of letter and number recognition.

Rectangles

Find and cross out the object that is **not** a **rectangle**.

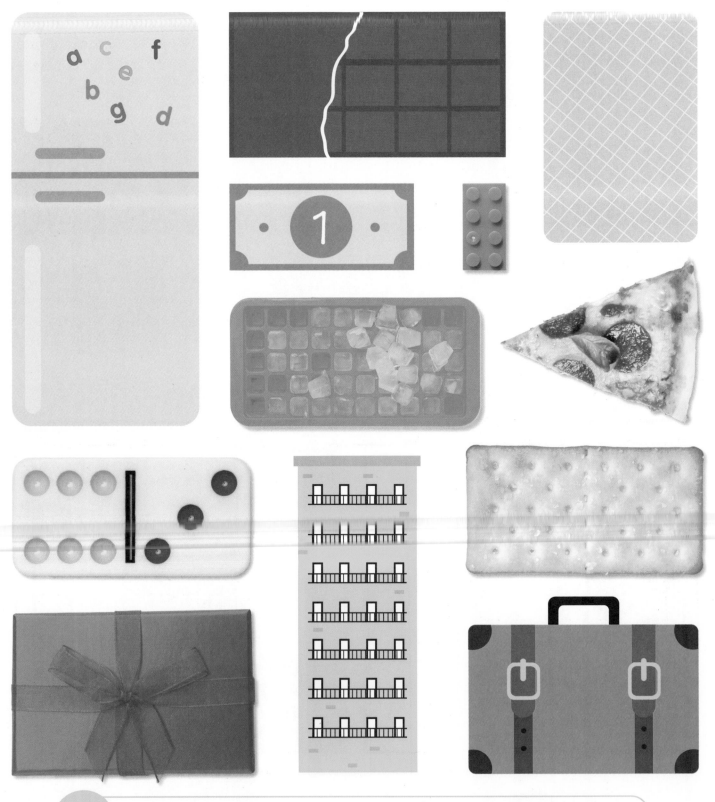

TOP TIP Explain to your child that rectangles have two long sides of the same length and two short sides of the same length. Count the sides together.

146

Rectangles

Trace the **rectangles**.

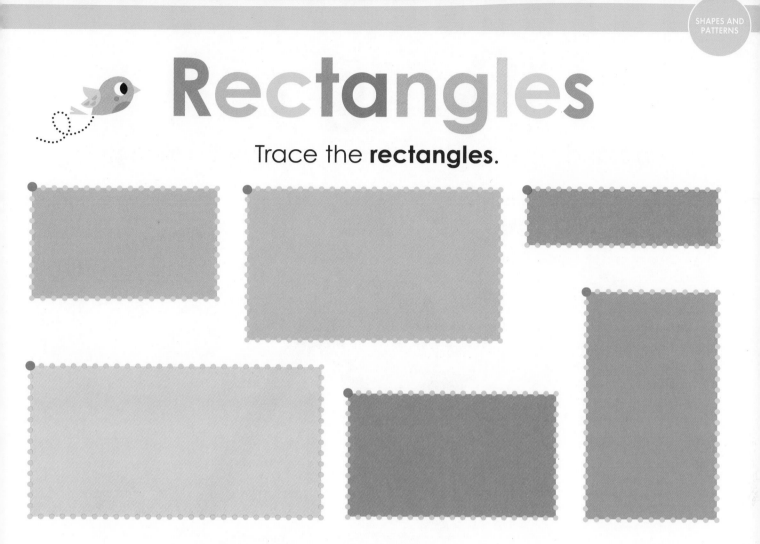

Color the big rectangles **red** and the small rectangles **blue**.

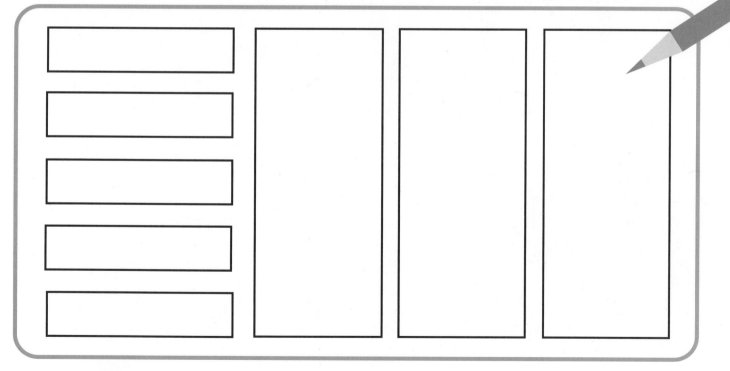

TOP TIP Learning about shapes helps develop your child's observational skills and is a great way to practice identifying similarities and differences.

Triangles

Find and cross out the object that is **not** a **triangle**.

TOP TIP   Ask your child to find some triangle shapes on your television remote control.

148

Triangles

Trace the **triangles**.

Complete the **triangle** pattern.

Stars

Find and cross out the object that is **not** a **star**.

Stars

Trace the **stars**.

Color Ella's star **green** and Aiden's star **yellow**.

TOP TIP Shape activities, such as seeing which shapes fit together using blocks or tiles, can help develop your child's problem-solving abilities.

151

Circles

Find and cross out the object that is **not** a **circle**.

TOP TIP Draw some circles with your child, demonstrating how to start at the top, move in a counterclockwise direction, and finish at the same point.

152

Circles

Trace the **circles**.

Complete the **circle** pattern.

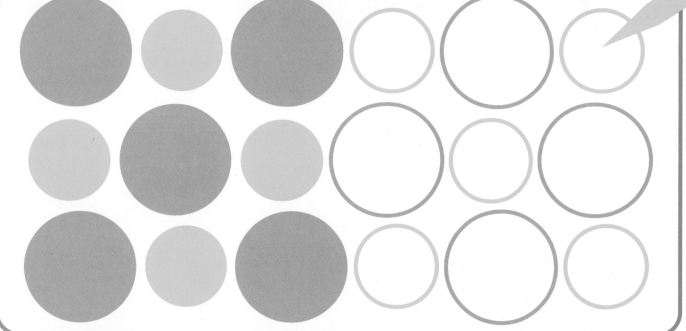

TOP TIP When talking about shapes with your child, encourage him or her to use descriptive words such as *big* or *small*, *red* or *green*.

Hearts

Find and cross out the object that is **not** a **heart**.

TOP TIP Together, make and decorate a card featuring hearts to give to a family member or friend.

Hearts

Trace the **hearts**.

Color the big hearts **purple** and the small hearts **orange**.

TOP TIP Ask your child to trace the shape of a heart with his or her index finger before tracing it with a pencil.

155

Ovals

Find and cross out the object that is **not** an **oval**.

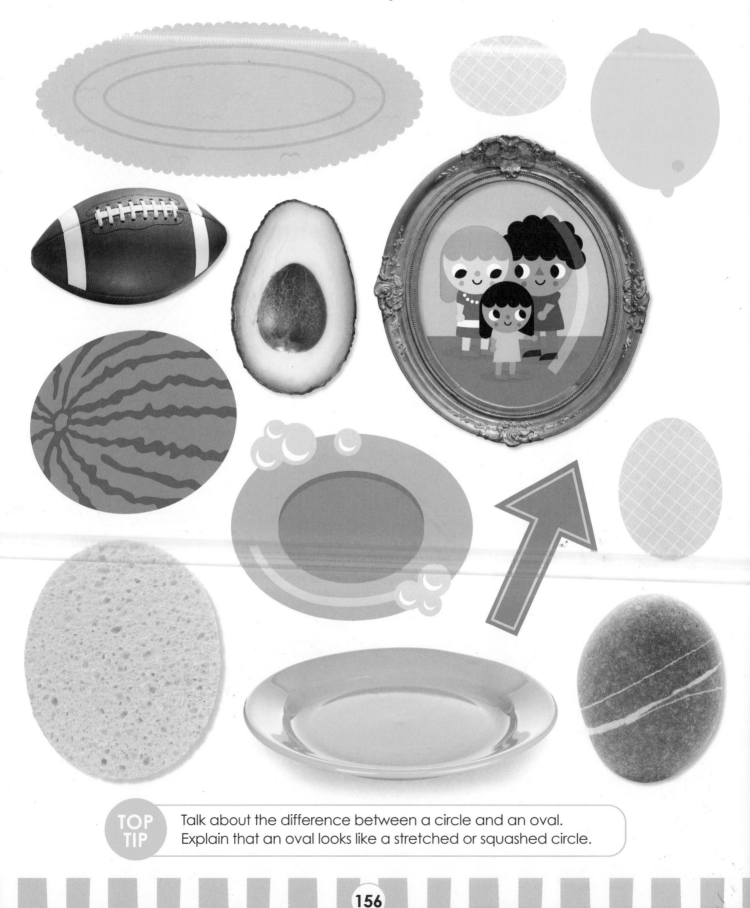

Talk about the difference between a circle and an oval.
Explain that an oval looks like a stretched or squashed circle.

Ovals

Trace the **ovals**.

Finish coloring these patterned eggs.

Draw a series of blank ovals on a piece of paper. Ask your child to get creative by adding to them—one could be a fish, another a pond, another a balloon.

Matching shapes

Draw lines to join the shapes that are the same.

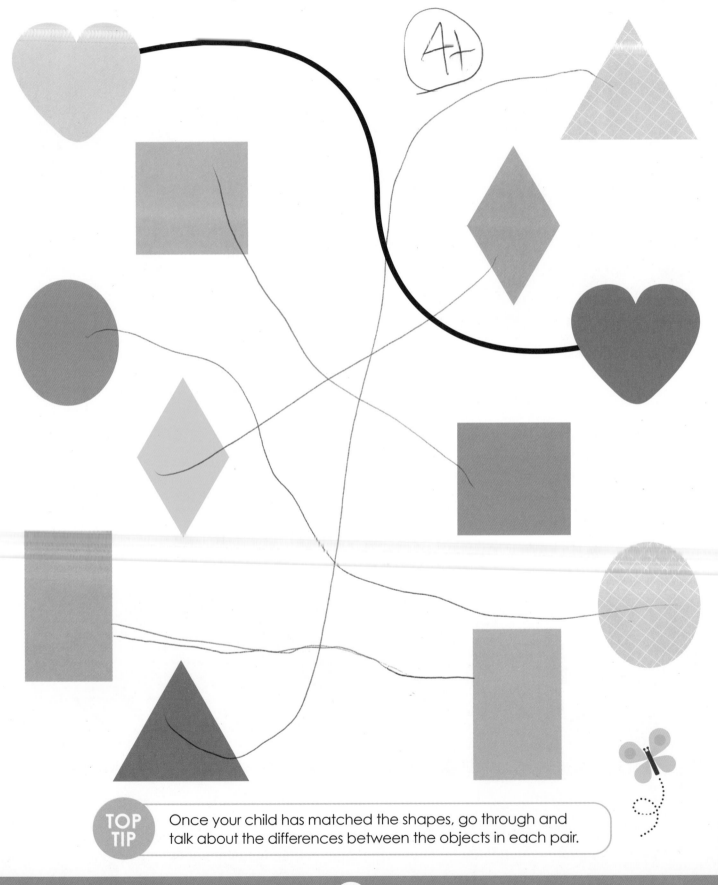

TOP TIP Once your child has matched the shapes, go through and talk about the differences between the objects in each pair.

Matching objects

Draw lines to link the objects to the correct shape.

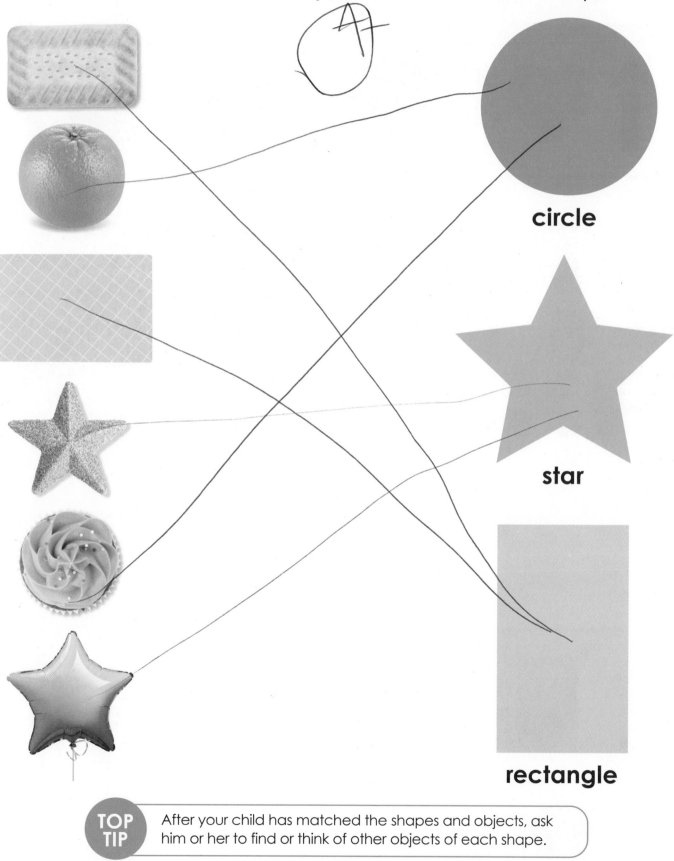

circle

star

rectangle

Shape patterns

Circle the picture that comes next in each row.

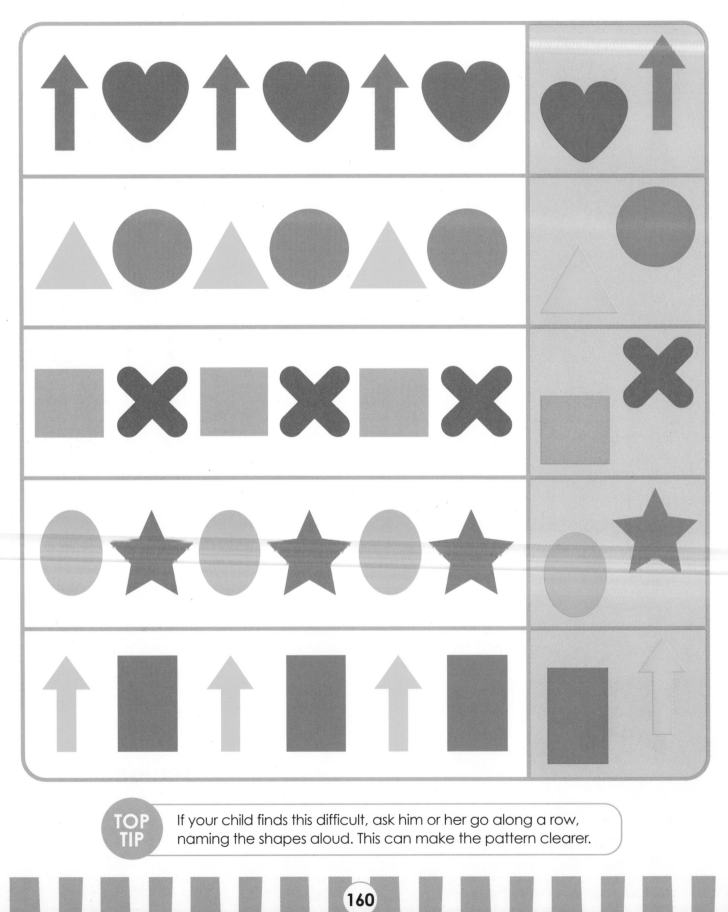

Picture patterns

Circle the picture that comes next in each row.

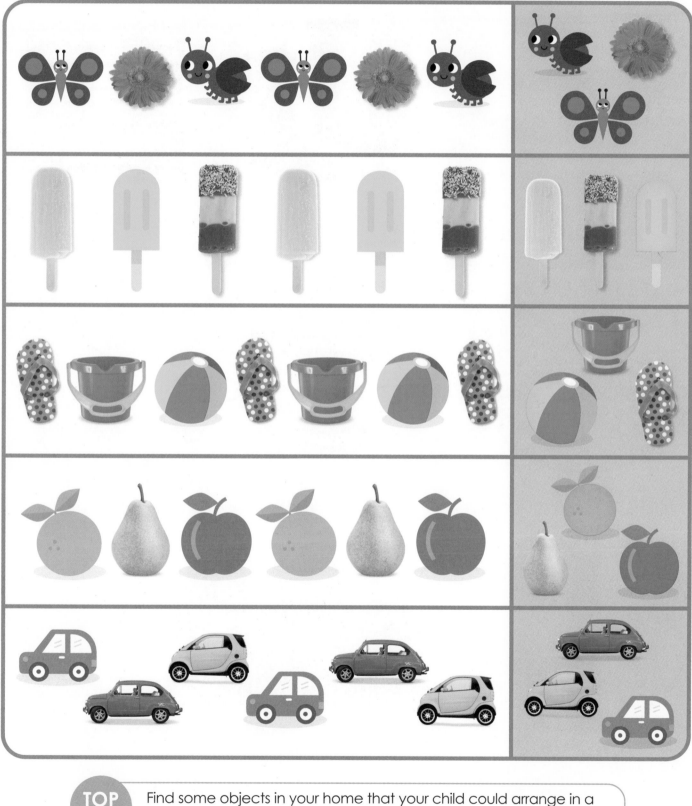

Find some objects in your home that your child could arrange in a pattern. Pieces of fruit, colored blocks, or crayons could work well.

Patterns at home

Match the patterns to the objects you might find at home.

stripes

spots

checks

TOP TIP Together, go through your child's clothes and talk about any items that have patterns.

Mosaic

Shapes fit together to make patterns.
Color each shape a different color.

TOP TIP Talk about and name the different shapes that appear in the mosaic.
Look for similar patterns in floor or wall coverings or on fabrics.

Match vehicles

Draw lines to match the vehicles.

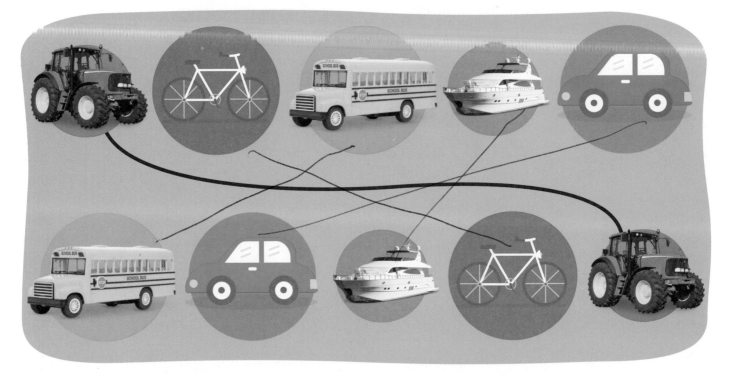

Draw lines to match the trucks.

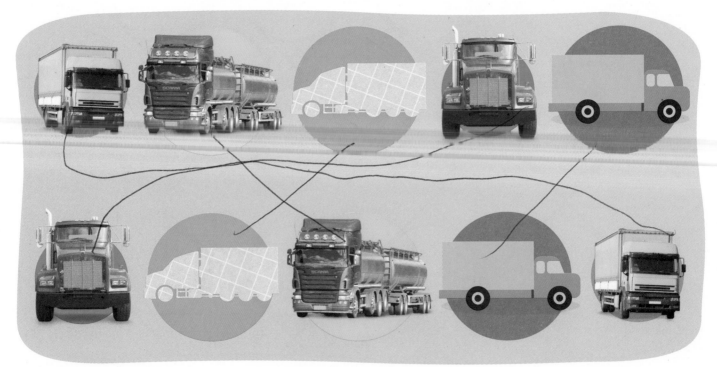

TOP TIP The trucks in the second activity are more similar to one another than the vehicles in the first activity. This encourages increasing attention to detail.

Match pets

Draw lines to match the cats.

Draw lines to match the dogs.

TOP TIP Sorting is a skill that children need for both math and science. It is a first step in learning to find similarities and differences between objects.

Pair the socks

Draw lines to match the socks.

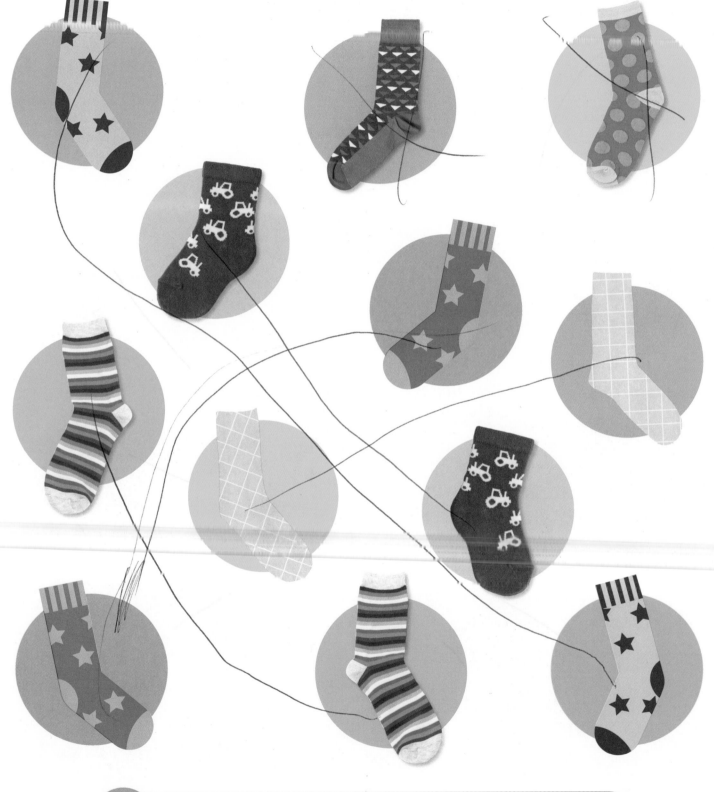

Shorts and tops

Draw lines to match the T-shirts with the shorts of the same color.

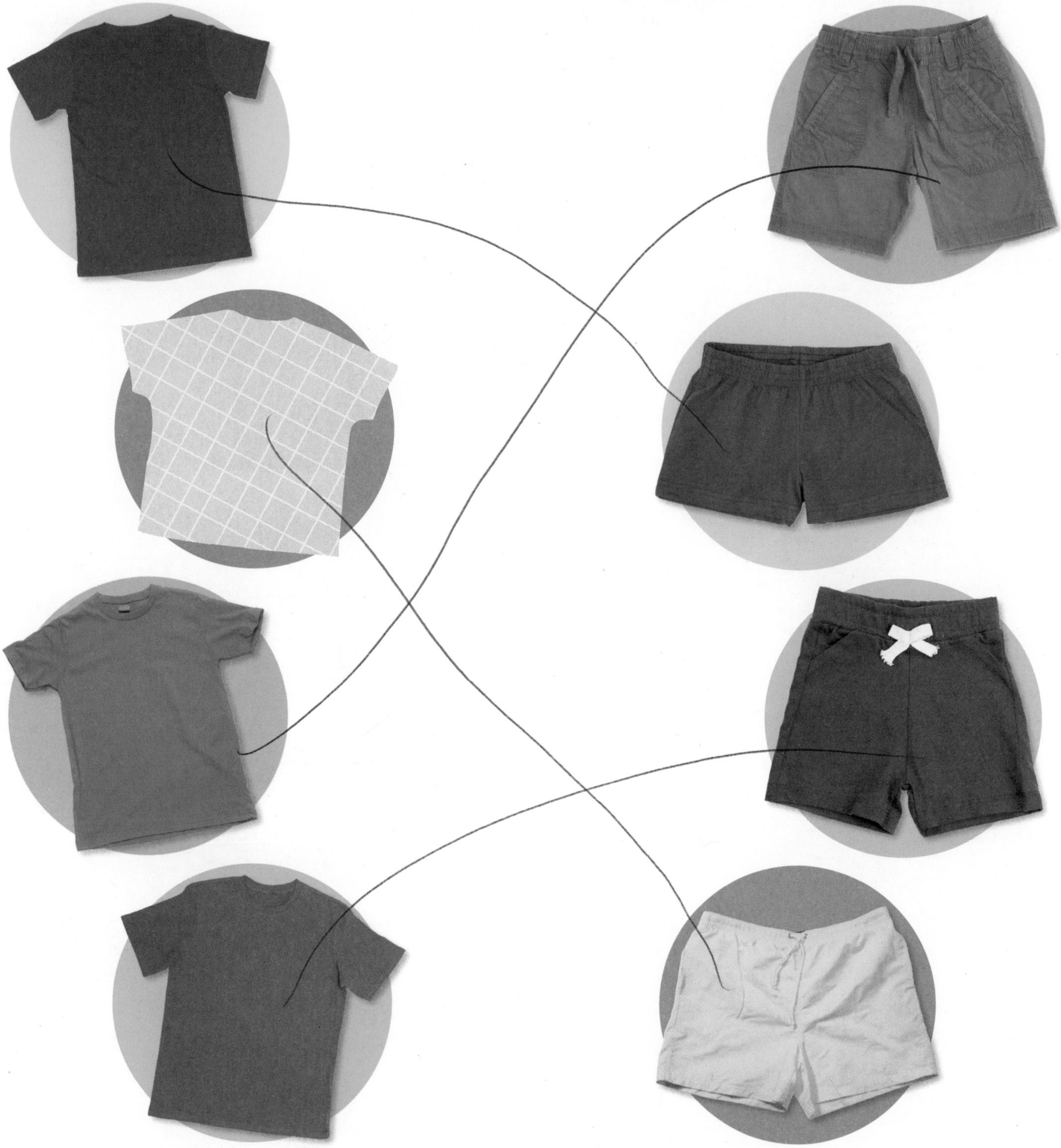

TOP
TIP

Sorting activities help a child's brain development by building memory, focus, and problem-solving skills.

Find the pairs

Draw lines to match the things that are the same.

Find the pairs

Draw lines to match the things that are the same.

TOP TIP This activity is slightly more complex than the previous activity because children need to find both objects within the scene.

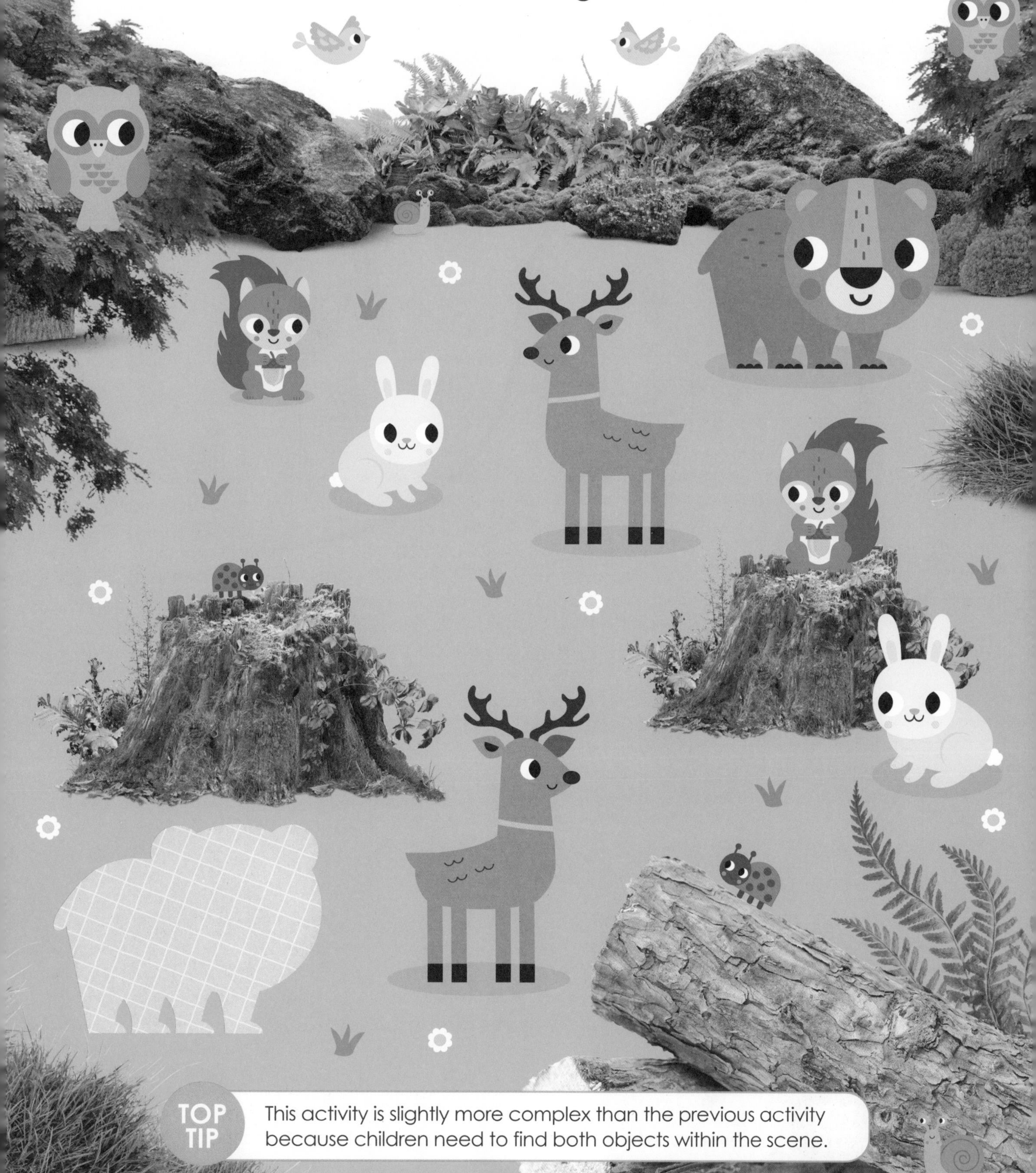

Pair the birds

Draw lines to match the birds with their partners.

TOP TIP Help your child by explaining that the males and females of some species look similar but are not identical to one another.

Crabs and beetles

Draw lines from the crabs to the big crab.
Draw lines from the beetles to the big beetle.

TOP TIP If your child needs help with this activity, encourage him or her to focus on details such as the number of legs or whether claws are present.

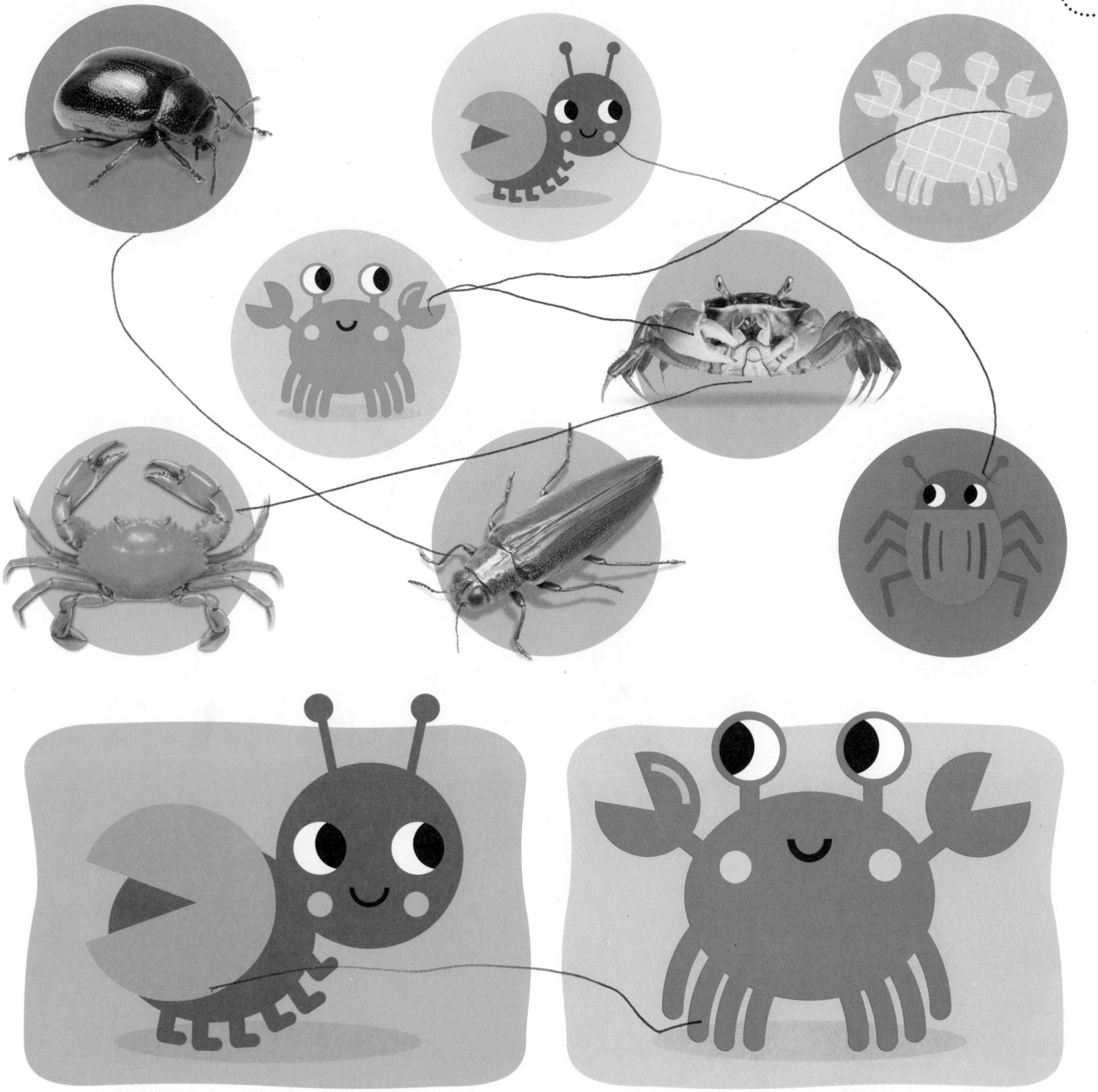

Whose job?

Draw lines to match the workers to their equipment.

TOP TIP This activity involves thinking about what each person uses to do their job, not just comparing pictures. Help your child identify each job.

172

Whose home?

Draw lines to match the animals to their homes.

TOP TIP In science, many tasks involve classifying objects and finding relationships between them. Activities such as this provide a first step.

173

Sort clothes

Draw lines from the sweaters to the sweater drawer.
Draw lines from the pants to the pants drawer.

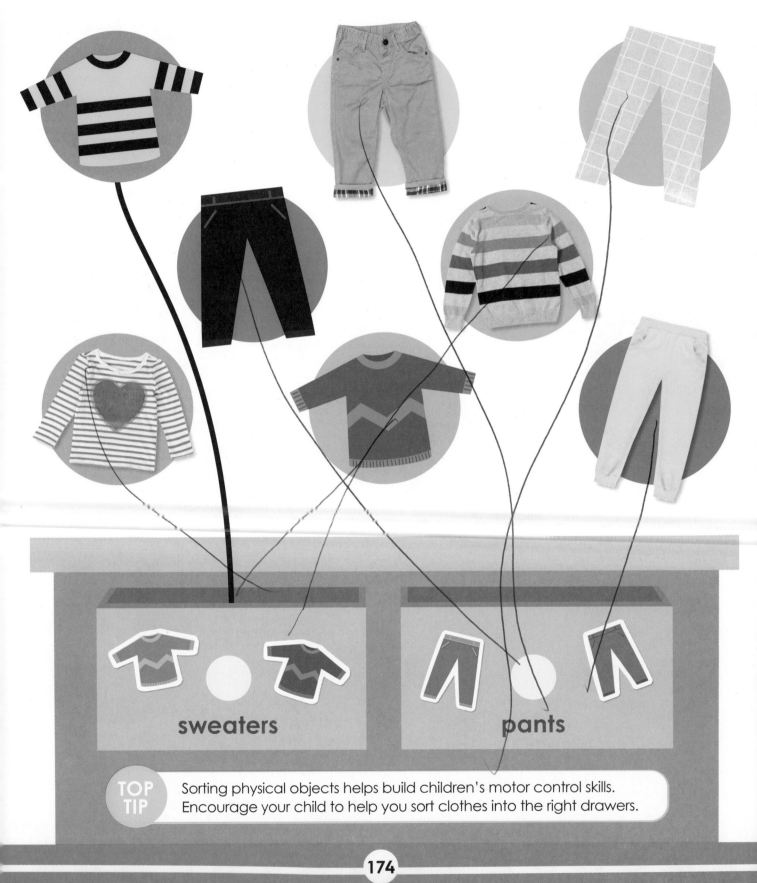

sweaters

pants

TOP TIP Sorting physical objects helps build children's motor control skills. Encourage your child to help you sort clothes into the right drawers.

SORTING

Sort toys

Draw lines from the blocks to the blocks box.
Draw lines from the stuffed toys to the stuffed toys box.

stuffed toys

blocks

TOP TIP Provide your child with labeled containers for sorting and storing toys. This has the added benefit of keeping your home more organized!

175

What's different?

Circle the one that's different in each row.

TOP TIP Help your child identify the group that four of the five objects in each row belong to. Give prompts only if necessary.

What's different?

Circle the one that's different in each row.

Here, the objects in each row are more similar than on the last page. This will encourage your child to focus more closely on detail.

What's wrong?

Cross out the things that don't belong in the kitchen.

TOP TIP This activity involves finding objects within a scene. Make it fun for your child by laughing about the things that shouldn't be there.

What's wrong?

Cross out the things that don't belong in the backyard.

TOP TIP You could extend this activity by discussing reasons for why each crossed-out object shouldn't be kept in a backyard.

179

Match opposites

Draw lines to match each thing to its opposite.

awake

on

rainy

cold

asleep

sunny

clean

off

hot

dirty

TOP TIP Learning about opposites is a fun introduction to antonyms. It builds word knowledge and higher-order thinking skills.

Sort into three

Draw lines from each food to the matching colored dot.

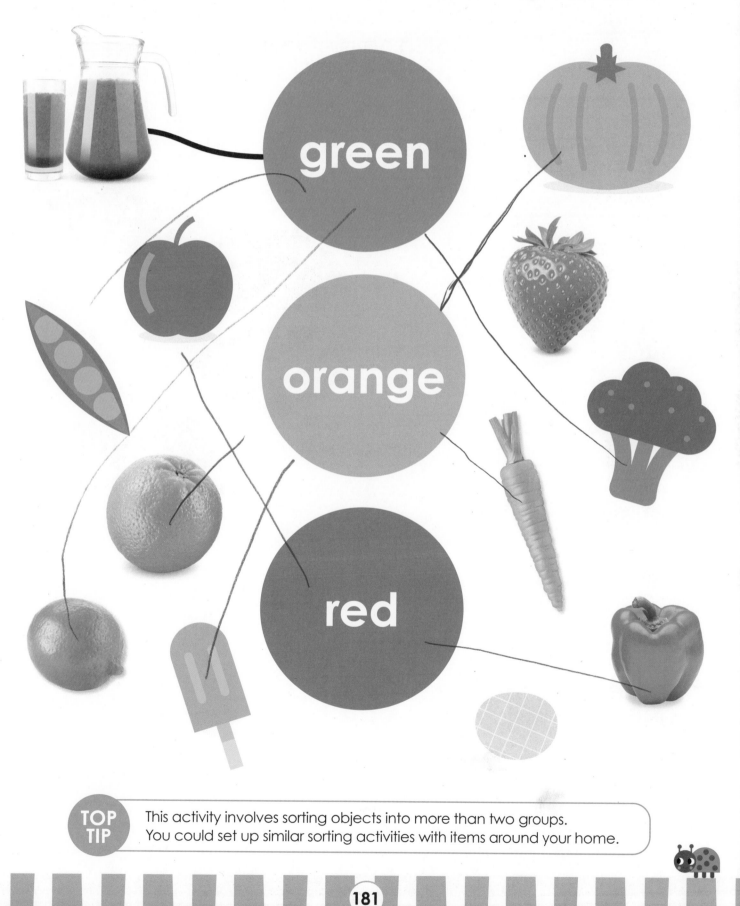

green

orange

red

Our needs

People need four things to stay alive: water, food, air, and shelter. Trace the words, and then draw lines to the matching pictures.

water

air

food

shelter

TOP TIP Discuss the four basic needs with your child. Talk about how your family acquires these essentials.

Five senses

We use our senses to find out about the world around us. Trace the body parts, and then trace the lines to match them with the senses.

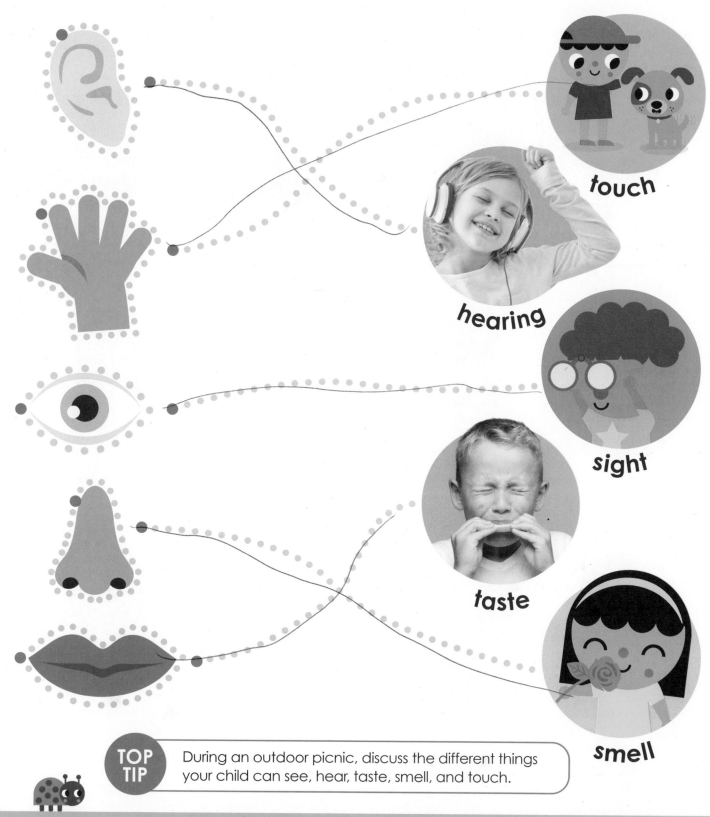

touch

hearing

sight

taste

smell

TOP TIP During an outdoor picnic, discuss the different things your child can see, hear, taste, smell, and touch.

Living things

Real plants need water and sunshine to live and grow.
Real animals need water and food to live and grow.
Circle the living thing in each pair.

TOP TIP Talk about the pros and cons of owning a real cat or dog compared with a toy one. Discuss the care that real animals need.

Animal babies

Baby animals often look like their parents, but they are smaller. Draw lines to match the babies with their parents.

TOP TIP Visit an animal park or open farm in spring so that your child can see the baby animals. Compare the babies with the adults.

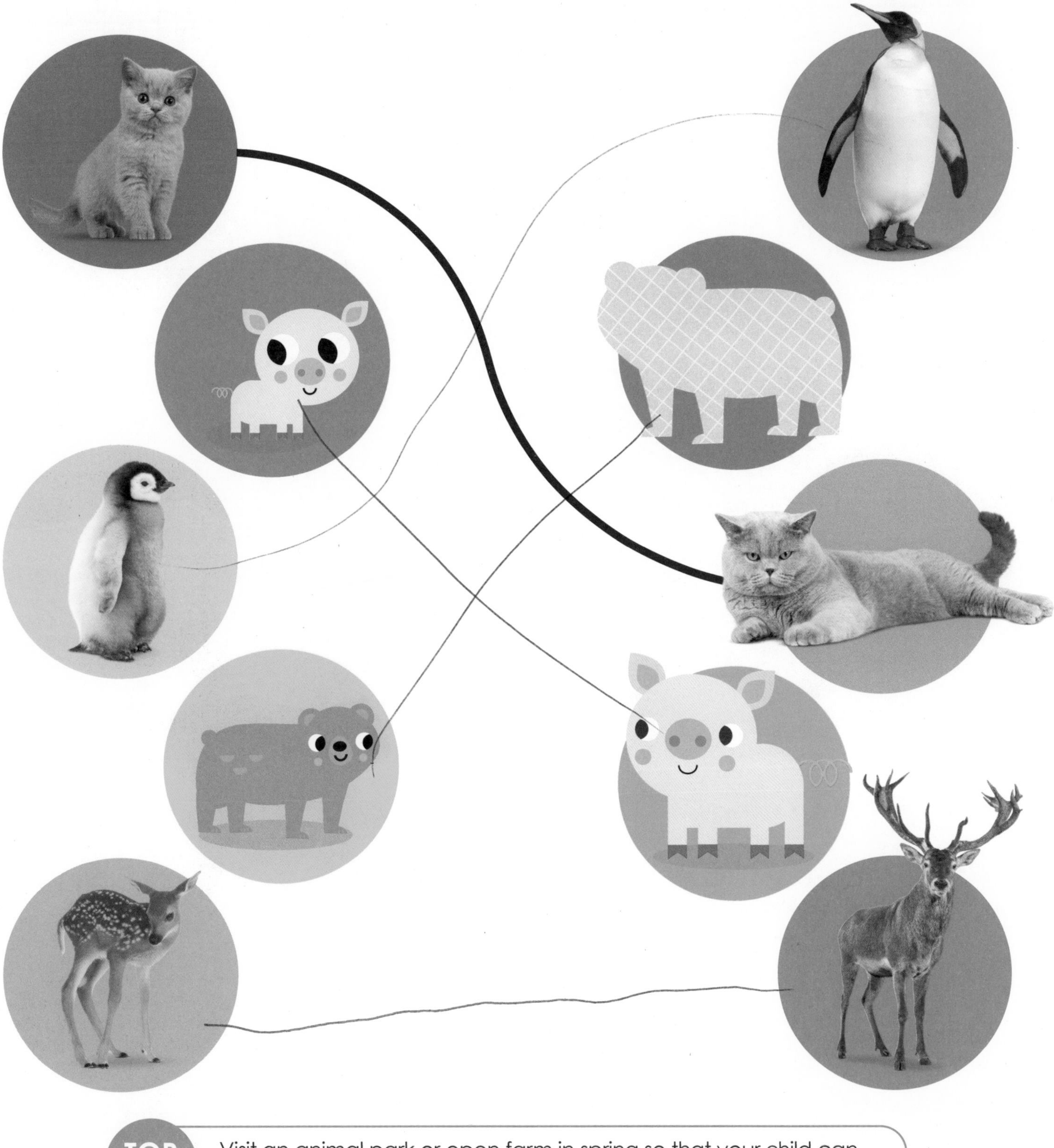

Animal homes

Animals need food, water, air, and shelter, just like people.
Draw lines to match the animals to their shelters.

TOP TIP When visiting an animal park or open farm, discuss how each type of shelter suits the animals living in it.

Plants

Plants provide us with many foods. Draw lines to match each plant with the food it provides.

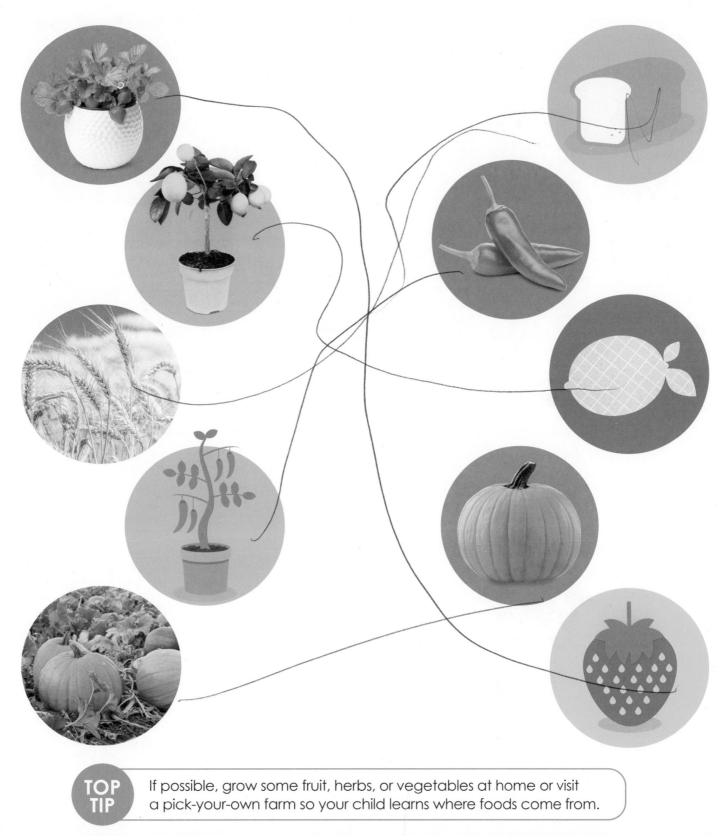

TOP TIP If possible, grow some fruit, herbs, or vegetables at home or visit a pick-your-own farm so your child learns where foods come from.

Planet Earth

Write an **L** by the pictures of dry land.
Write a **W** by the pictures of water.

Planet Earth is round
like a ball.
Color the oceans blue
and the land green.

TOP TIP Together, look at a globe or map and locate places of importance to your family.

The Sun

The Sun is a star that is close to Earth.
Sticker and finish coloring these pictures that show
how the Sun helps us.

The Sun is hot and keeps us warm.

The Sun gives us light. It lets us see.

The Sun helps our crops grow.

The Sun helps us dry things.

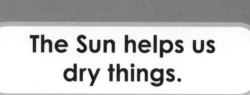

TOP TIP On a sunny day, conduct an experiment comparing how quickly ice melts in direct sun and in shade.

The Moon

The Moon is a big rocky ball that circles around Earth.
Some nights we see more of the Moon than other nights.
Trace these pictures of the Moon.

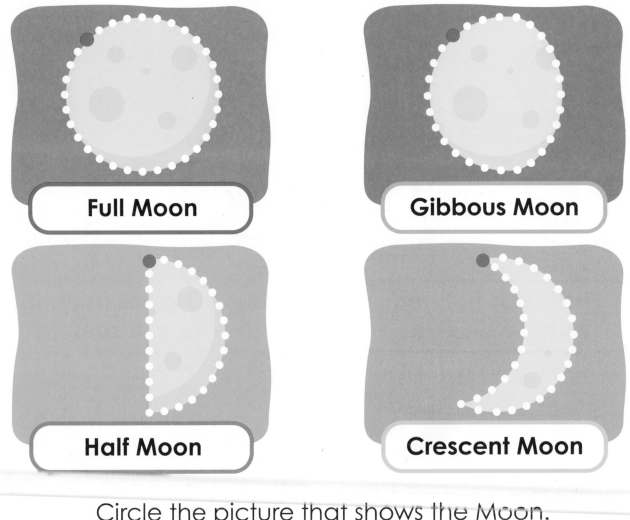

Full Moon

Gibbous Moon

Half Moon

Crescent Moon

Circle the picture that shows the Moon.

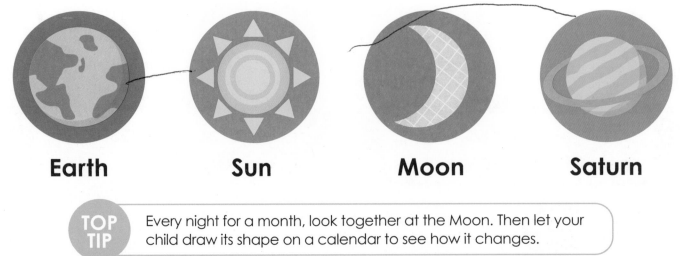

Earth   **Sun**   **Moon**   **Saturn**

TOP TIP Every night for a month, look together at the Moon. Then let your child draw its shape on a calendar to see how it changes.

Day and night

Trace the words. Then draw lines from the daytime pictures to the Sun and from the nighttime pictures to the Moon.

owl   **picnic**   **closed flower**   **pigeon**

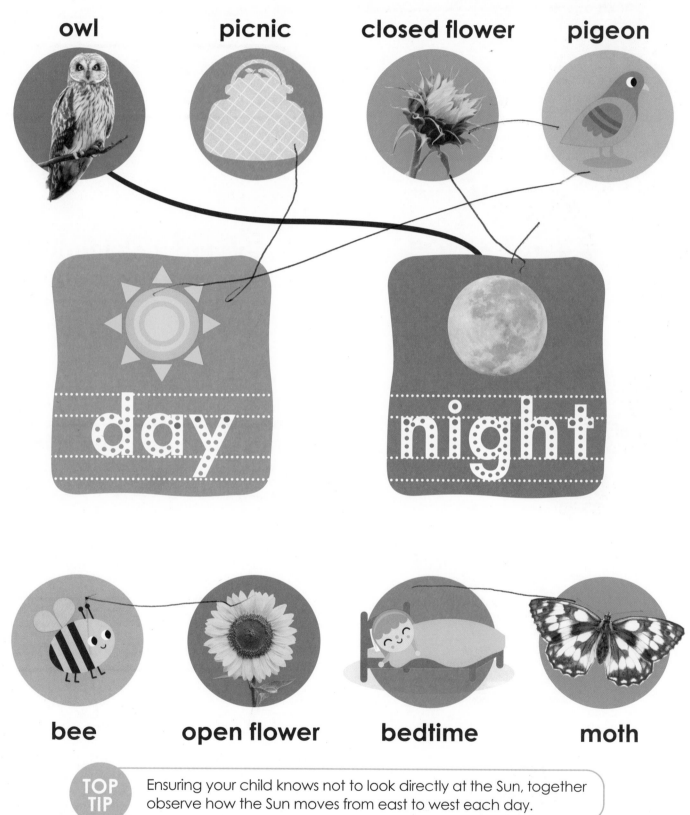

day

night

bee   **open flower**   **bedtime**   **moth**

TOP TIP Ensuring your child knows not to look directly at the Sun, together observe how the Sun moves from east to west each day.

Rocks

Draw lines to match the rocks with the sentences.

This white rock is made of salt.

This red rock formed deep under the ground.

This rock with fossils in it formed under the sea.

This black shiny rock came from a volcano.

TOP TIP Use a magnifying glass to look at different rocks. Discuss their colors, textures, and other features.

Wood or plastic?

Wood comes from the trunks and branches of trees.
Plastic is made in factories. It is made in many colors.
Circle the object in each pair that is made of wood.

TOP TIP Discuss the different pros and cons of each material, including weight, color, and environmental issues.

Glass or metal?

People make glass from melted sand. We get metals from under the ground. Put a check by each glass object.

TOP TIP Talk about the properties of the materials. For example, how glass is see-through but easily broken and how metal is strong.

194

Sink or float?

Some things float on top of water. Other things sink to the bottom. Trace the words, and then draw a line from each object to the correct word.

float

sink

TOP TIP Conduct a floating and sinking experiment with a bowl of water. Ask your child to guess what will happen with each object before it is tested.

195

Soft or hard?

Circle the object in each pair that is soft.

TOP TIP Ask your child to sort a group of objects into hard and soft sets.
Then discuss the advantages to the objects being hard or soft.

196

 SCIENCE

Quiet or loud?

Put a check by each noisy object.

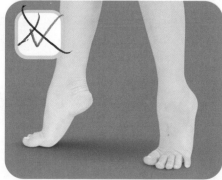

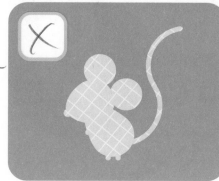

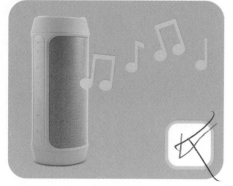

TOP TIP Discuss times and places where it is okay to be noisy and times and places where we should keep quiet.

Cold or hot?

Color the word hot **red** and the word cold **blue**.
Then draw lines from each picture to the correct word.

hot

cold

TOP TIP Talk about when you like to eat hot or cold foods.
Also, discuss the dangers of burning or getting too cold.

Dig or lift?

Write a **D** by the things we use to dig.
Write an **L** by the things we use to lift.

TOP TIP — If possible, provide your child with children's tools, gardening implements, or cutlery. Teach him or her how to use them safely and effectively.

Cut or join?

Write a **C** by the things we use to cut.
Write a **J** by the things we use to join or stick.

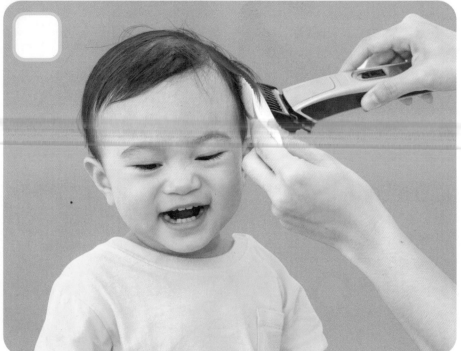

TOP TIP Create opportunities for your child to make things using boxes, tubes, safety scissors, string, and glue.

Heat or light?

Draw lines from the things that give us heat to the flame.
Draw lines from the things that give us light to the bulb.

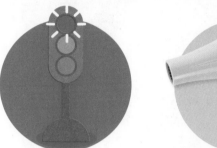

TOP TIP Take apart a simple flashlight and show your child how the batteries link to the bulb via wires. Allow your child to put it back together.

My name

Zoey and Luke have written their names.

Zoey

Luke

Draw your face, and then write your name.

My age

Count the candles and trace the numbers.
Then circle the child who is the same age as you.

I am ___LUKe___ years old.

My birthday

Circle the month you were born.

January	February	March	April
May	June	July	August
September	October	November	December

Circle the day of the month you were born.

1 2 3 4 5 6 7 8 9 10 11

12 13 14 15 16 17 18 19 20 21 22

23 24 25 26 27 28 29 30 31

I was born on _____ [month]

_____ [day], _____ [year].

On my next birthday,

I will be _____ years old.

TOP TIP Teaching your child his or her birthday date increases awareness of time, days, dates, and years.

My body

Add the stickers to complete the girl's body.

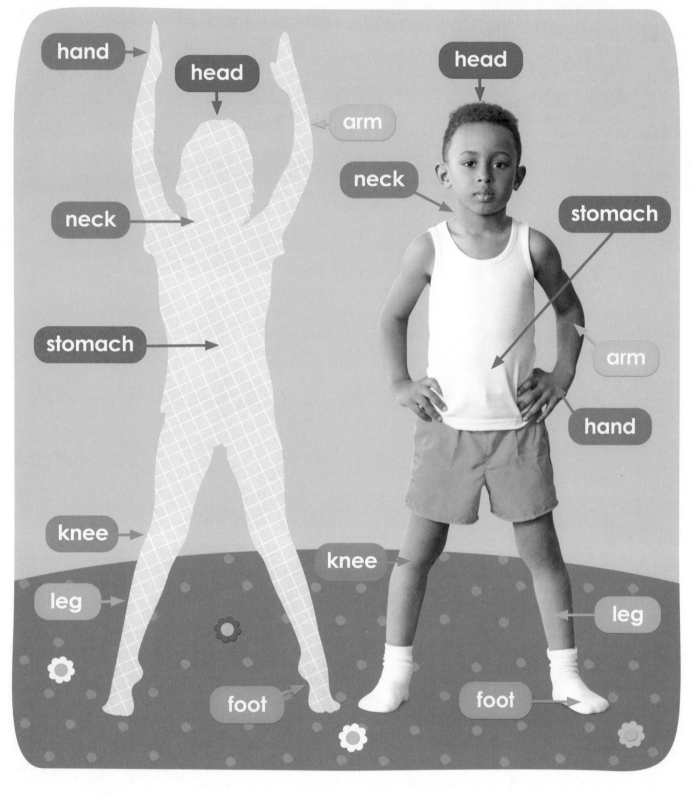

TOP TIP To prepare for this activity, play a game of Simon Says where you ask your child to point to the different parts of his or her body.

My family

Some families are big, and some are small.
Draw your family in the park scene.

Count the people in your family and
write the number in the box.

TOP TIP Together, look at photos of extended family members to help your child
remember the names and faces of those you don't see often.

My friends

Draw pictures of your friends in the hearts.

Circle the activities you like to do with friends.

play in a park

play ball

share candy

dress up

play tag

jump

TOP TIP If possible, provide opportunities for your child to play with others of the same age. Friendships help build good communication and social skills.

My home

Circle the type of home you live in.

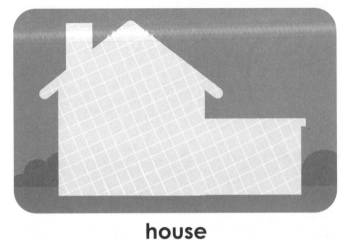

house

apartment

mobile home

cabin

Draw a picture of your home.

TOP TIP Point out different types of homes to your child and discuss their different advantages to help build his or her knowledge and vocabulary.

Where I live

Check the things that are in your neighborhood.

park

school

farm fields

supermarket

bus stop

laundromat

traffic lights

swimming pool

POST OFFICE

post office

TOP TIP Help your child memorize his or her home address and contact number. You could also discuss safe people to approach if lost.

My day

Trace the yellow lines.
Then check the things you do in your day.

wake up

get dressed

brush my hair

eat breakfast

brush my teeth

go to preschool

play outside

have a snack

eat lunch

watch TV

TOP TIP Teach your child about daily routines. Reward charts can be useful if he or she avoids an activity such as toothbrushing.

My night

Trace the blue lines.
Then check the things you do in the evening.

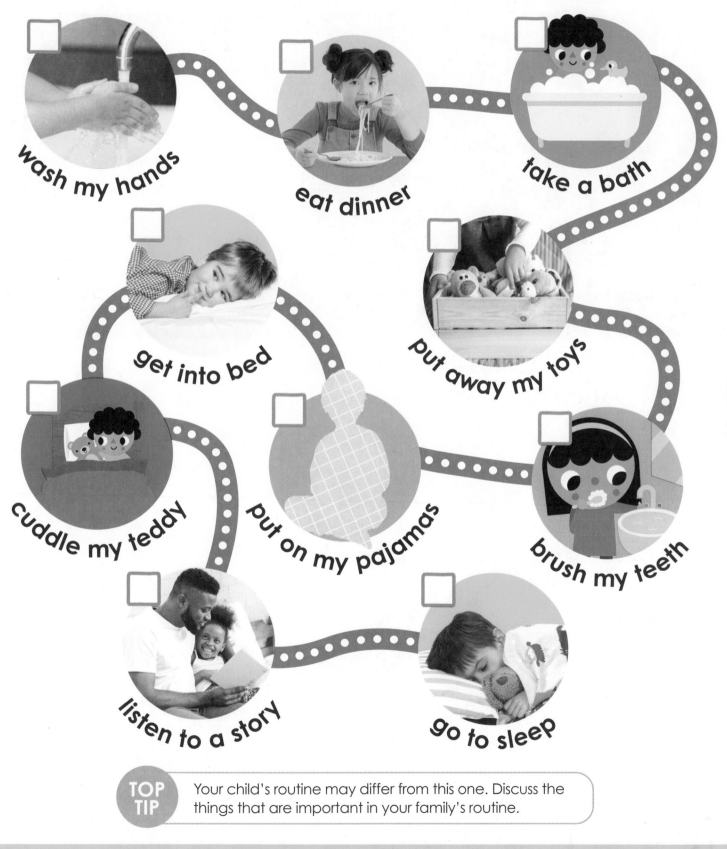

wash my hands

eat dinner

take a bath

get into bed

put away my toys

cuddle my teddy

put on my pajamas

brush my teeth

listen to a story

go to sleep

TOP TIP Your child's routine may differ from this one. Discuss the things that are important in your family's routine.

My meals

Circle the breakfast foods you like.
Then draw your favorite breakfast on the plate.

cereal   **oatmeal**   **waffles**

toast   **eggs**   **bacon**

Circle the dinner foods you like.
Then draw your favorite dinner on the plate.

rice   **vegetables**   **burger**

pasta   **chicken**   **taco**

TOP TIP Rather than talking about foods as bad or good, discuss which foods help us grow strong and give us energy.

My snacks

Draw a line from each snack to where it came from.

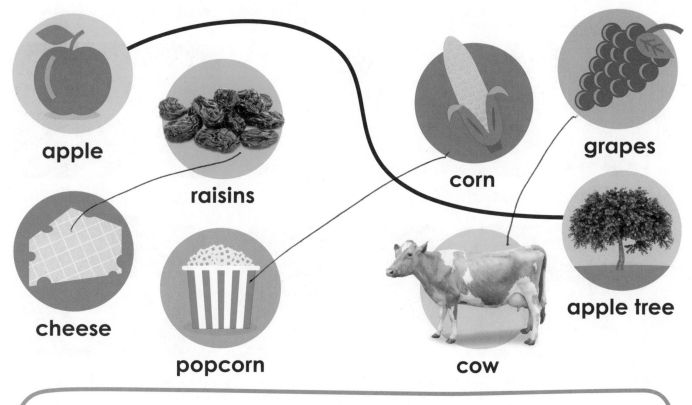

apple

raisins

cheese

popcorn

corn

cow

grapes

apple tree

Draw your favorite snack in the box.

This is my _____.

TOP TIP Use mealtimes to teach your child about where different foods come from. If on a journey, point out different types of farms.

I stay healthy

Circle the pictures that show healthy activities.
Cross out the unhealthy activities.

I wash my hands.

I do exercise.

I don't wash off dirt.

I get plenty of sleep.

I eat only candy.

I eat lots of fruit.

Draw yourself doing something healthy.

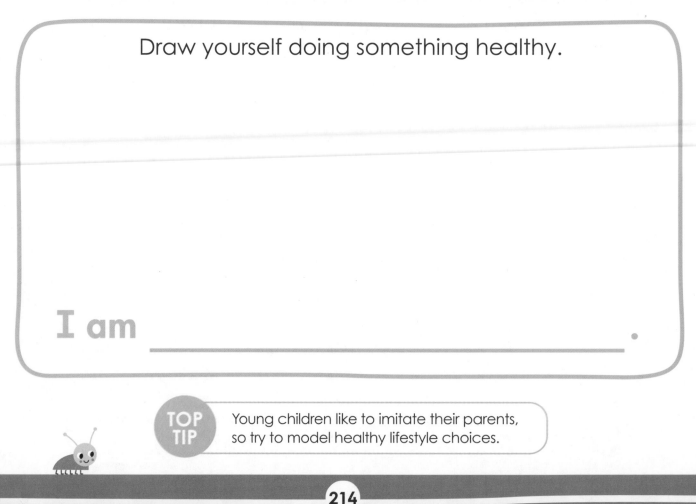

I am _____.

TOP TIP Young children like to imitate their parents, so try to model healthy lifestyle choices.

My toys

Circle the toys you like to play with.

doll

train

bubbles

yo-yo

bike

modeling clay

drum

computer game

Draw your favorite toy in the box.

This is my _____.

TOP TIP Exposing your child to a variety of toys helps develop different skills, including fine motor control and hand-eye co-ordination.

When I need help

Draw lines to show who helps us in each situation.

feeling sick

building on fire

doctor

police officer

mechanic

getting lost

broken-down car

firefighter

What number do you call in an emergency?
Write the number here:

TOP TIP Use this opportunity to gently discuss stranger danger and how to recognize safe people to talk to.

When I grow up

Check the boxes by the jobs you would like to do.
You can check as many as you like.

builder

chef

doctor

actor

teacher

scientist

artist

farmer

What job do you want to do when
you grow up? Draw it here.

I want to be a _____.

TOP TIP Discuss the importance of different jobs with your child. Show how the various roles come together to make our society function.

Being kind

Circle the kind actions. Cross out the unkind ones.

sharing toys

leaving someone out

helping a friend

giving a gift

taking someone's toys

talking to someone lonely

Draw a picture of you being kind to someone else.

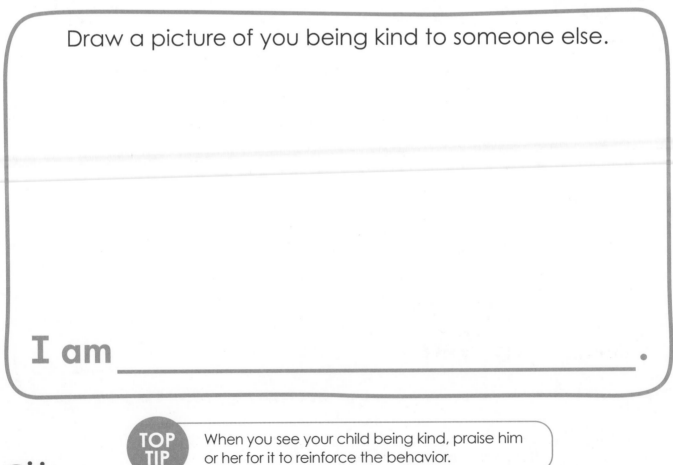

I am _____.

My enviroment

Trace the words and finish coloring the pictures.

I **reduce** wasted electricity by turning off lights when I'm not using them.

reduce

I **reuse** my water bottle instead of throwing it away.

reuse

I put things in **recycling** bins so the materials can be used again.

recycle

TOP TIP Encourage your child to help you sort the recycling. Discuss how each material is reused to make new things of the same material.

Good morning!

At kindergarten, your teacher will take care of you.
Trace the greetings these children give their teacher.

TOP TIP Inform your child that in kindergarten, he or she must follow the teacher's instructions and should tell the teacher if any problems arise.

220

Keep it here

You may have a cubby or closet for storing your bag and coat. Color the hats, coat, and boots in this picture.

TOP TIP Prepare your child for using a cubby by creating accessible places for him or her to store a backpack and coat at home.

Roll call

Your teacher will want to make sure you are at school. Trace Jack's reply when his teacher calls out his name.

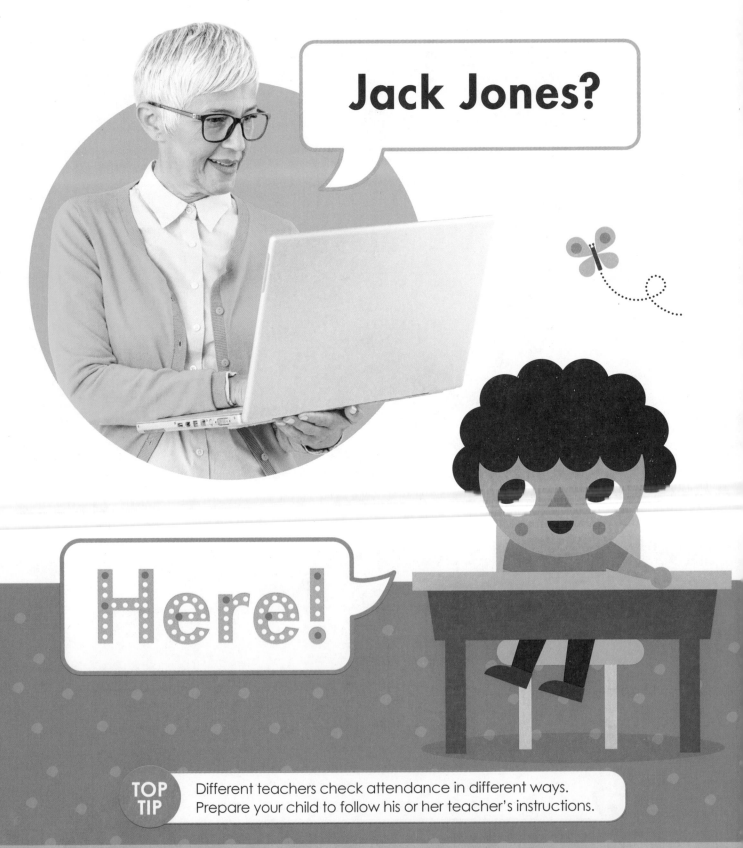

Jack Jones?

Here!

TOP TIP Different teachers check attendance in different ways. Prepare your child to follow his or her teacher's instructions.

Today's plan

Your teacher might let you know the schedule for the day.
Put the abacus sticker by the word Math.
Put the lunchbox sticker by the word Lunch.
Put the paintbrush sticker by the word Art.

9:00 Reading

11:30 Writing

2:00 Art

10:00 Math

12:00 Lunch

3:00 Home time

11:00 Recess

1:00 PE

TOP TIP Explain that the teacher will have a plan for the day. Many children like to know what is coming up and enjoy a regular routine.

Show-and-tell

During show-and-tell, you can talk to your class or show them something. This boy is showing his class a birdhouse. In the box, draw something you'd like to show your class.

TOP TIP You could have a short show-and-tell session at home. Show an object and tell your child about it, and then let your child do the same.

Let's read

Your class might visit the school library.
Draw a picture of a book you would like to read.

TOP TIP Help build a love of reading with regular visits to a local library. Allow your child to select a variety of fiction and nonfiction books.

Writing time

Circle the things you use for writing.
Cross out the things you don't need for writing.

eraser

pencil

cactus

banana

composition book

teddy bear

Write your name on this line.

....

TOP TIP If you are teaching your child to write letters, teach the lowercase letters first (except for the first letter of the child's name).

226

Playtime

At recess, you might play outside. Find and circle two balls, a jump rope, and a slide in this recess scene.

TOP TIP Regular physical activity helps children focus in class and can even help regulate mood.

Let's count

In math class, you will learn to count to 100.
Circle the things you might use in math class.
Cross out the things you won't use in math class.

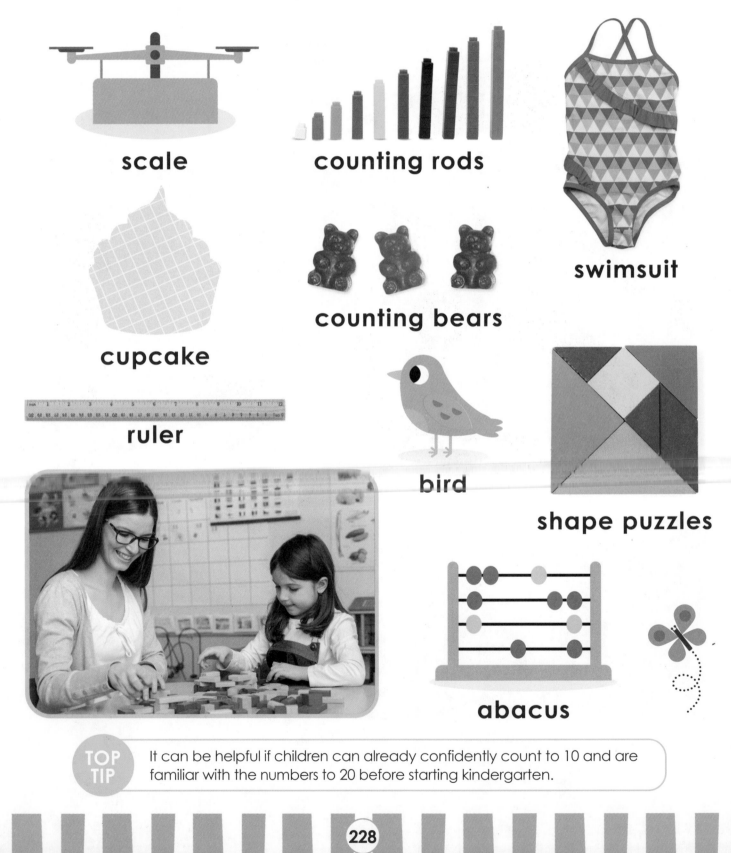

scale

counting rods

swimsuit

cupcake

counting bears

ruler

bird

shape puzzles

abacus

TOP TIP It can be helpful if children can already confidently count to 10 and are familiar with the numbers to 20 before starting kindergarten.

Make music

Sometimes you will sing and make music.
Circle the musical instruments.
Cross out the things that aren't instruments.

recorder

orange

drum

tambourine

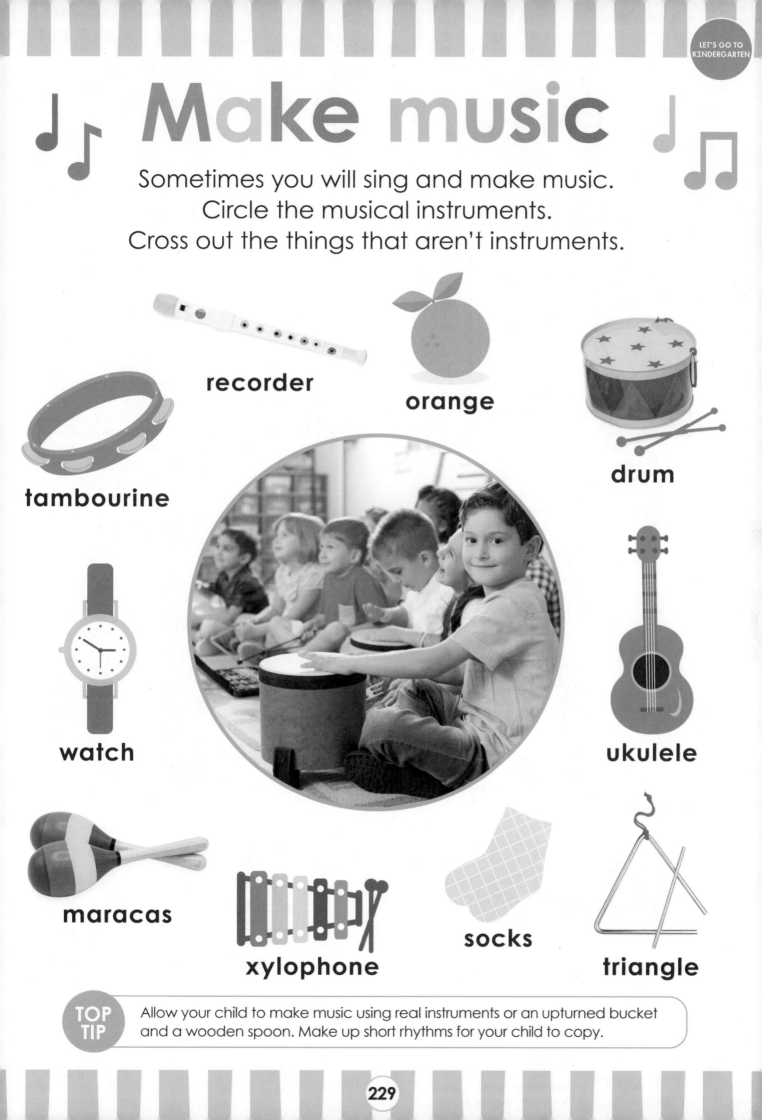

watch

ukulele

maracas

xylophone

socks

triangle

TOP TIP Allow your child to make music using real instruments or an upturned bucket and a wooden spoon. Make up short rhythms for your child to copy.

Computer time

You might do some work on a computer.
Color and sticker the computer equipment.

monitor

headphones

printer

tablet

mouse

laptop

keyboard

TOP TIP There are many free learning games online. Always check them first to make sure they are suitable for your child.

Story time

Sometimes your teacher will read you a book.
Draw lines from the labels to the parts of the diagram
that show how you should listen.

Put your hand up to talk.

Look at the book.

Use your ears to listen.

Talk when the teacher says you can.

Sit cross-legged.

Keep your hands in your lap.

TOP TIP One of the best ways to help develop a love of reading from a young age is with regular bedtime stories.

Science

You might learn about nature, our world, and space.
Circle the things you might do in science class.
Cross out the things you won't do in science class.

Do experiments

Take a nap

Learn about dinosaurs

Learn about insects

Eat your lunch

Learn about planets

Grow a plant

Make a boat

 TOP TIP Many children enjoy learning by doing. Look in a library or bookshop for science-activity books suitable for young children.

Lunchtime

You may have lunch at kindergarten. Some children bring a lunchbox from home. Others eat a cafeteria meal. Finish coloring Tom and Olivia's lunches.

MILK

TOP TIP If your child will be taking a lunchbox to kindergarten, have some picnic lunches using the lunchbox before he or she starts.

Make art

In art class, you will make things and draw or paint pictures.
Circle the things you might use in art class.
Cross out the things you won't use in art class.

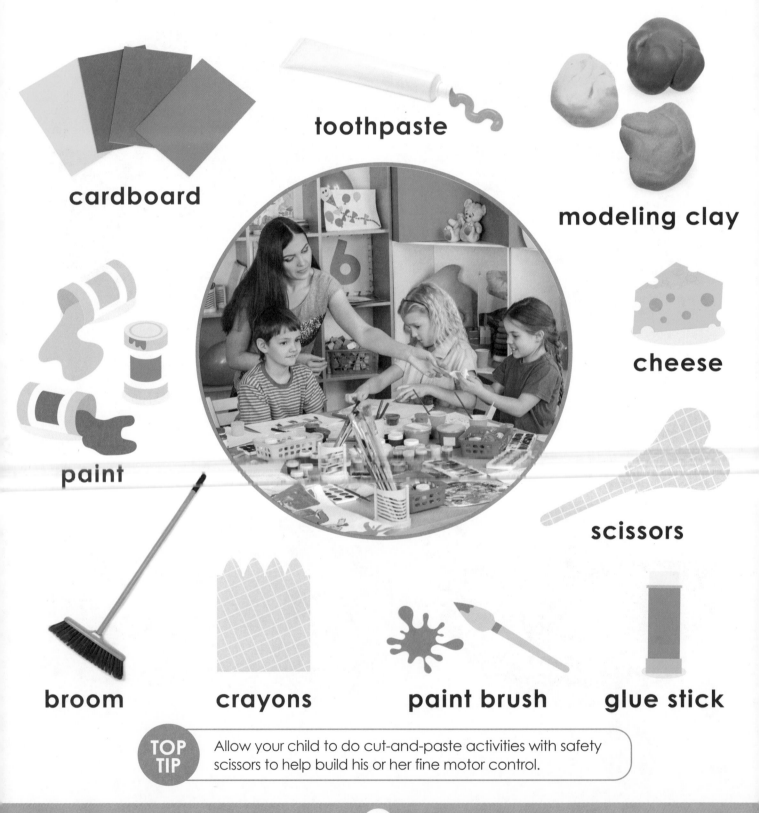

cardboard

toothpaste

modeling clay

cheese

paint

scissors

broom

crayons

paint brush

glue stick

TOP TIP Allow your child to do cut-and-paste activities with safety scissors to help build his or her fine motor control.

Put on a show

You might take part in a class concert or play.
Draw yourself in a fun costume on the stage below.

TOP TIP Encourage your child to join you in role-playing "at school" stories with toy characters.

Make friends

At kindergarten, you can make friends with other children.
Color and sticker this scene of friends playing together.

TOP TIP If your child worries about making friends on the first day, tell him or her that it can take time to form friendships and to just enjoy playing with others.

Class rules

Your class will have rules for you to follow.
Draw lines from the rules to the matching pictures.

Listen to the teacher.

Take turns.

Help others.

Walk, don't run.

Talk, don't shout.

Keep the room clean.

TOP TIP Try to use positive language when making rules (for example, say *stay in bed* rather than *don't get up*). Praise your child for obeying a rule.

Home time

Your class will pack up and get ready for home time.
Circle the things you take home from kindergarten
Cross out the things you leave at kindergarten.

coat

teacher

backpack

water bottle

table

reader

TOP TIP Talk to your child about how he or she will get home from kindergarten and what to do to keep safe.

Read at home

Your teacher may give you a reader to take home.
Sticker and color this picture of a child reading to his mom.

 TOP TIP If your child is ready, you could purchase some at-home readers, such as Scholastic's *First Little Readers* level A or the *Amazing Animals* box set.

Congratulations!

Good Work Award!

Name: Aluina   Mariah

has successfully completed the

Get Ready for
Kindergarten

Jumbo Workbook

Date: ....